AI DEEP DIVE

A HANDBOOK FOR IT PROFESSIONALS

MOHAMMED YOUSEF SHAIK

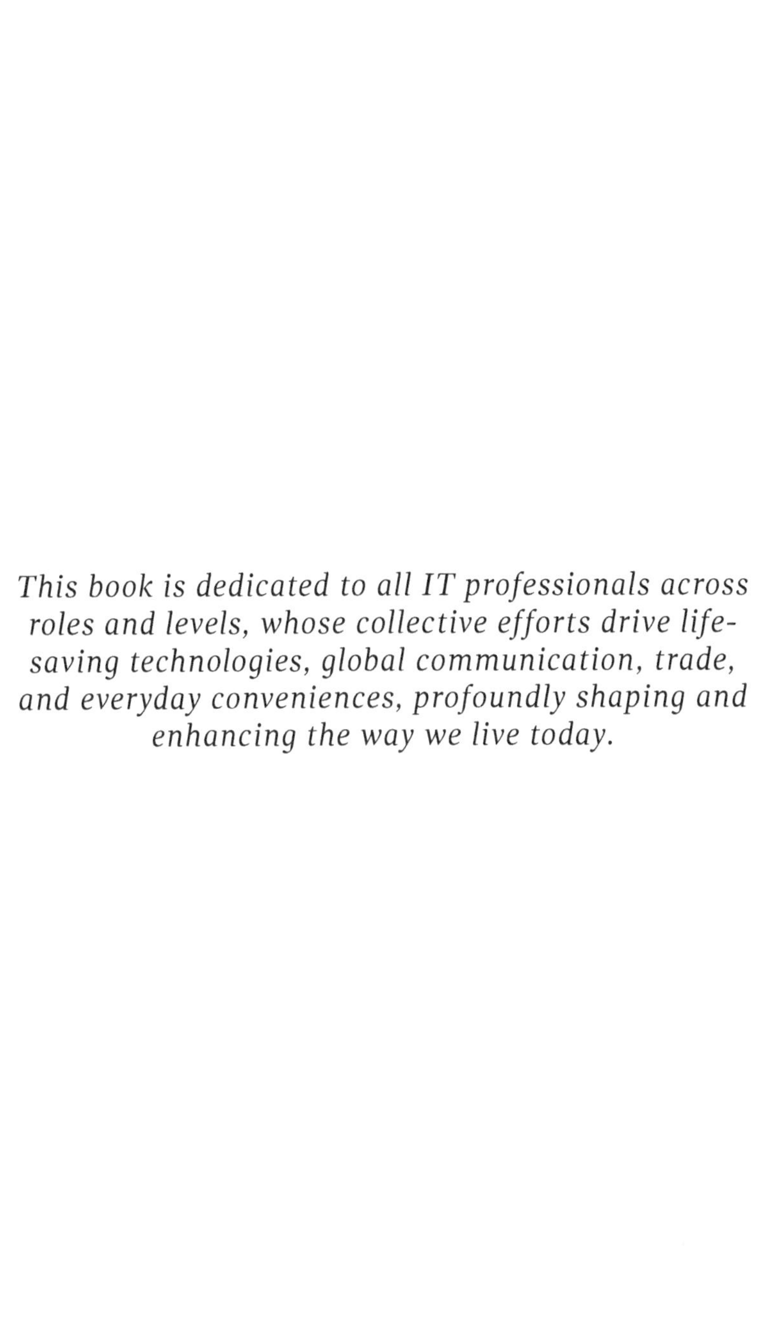

This book is dedicated to all IT professionals across roles and levels, whose collective efforts drive life-saving technologies, global communication, trade, and everyday conveniences, profoundly shaping and enhancing the way we live today.

Contents

Preface

In November 2024, Mohammed Yousef Shaik published a book
" **72 Years of Artificial Intelligence Innovation (1950-2022)** ",
a comprehensive exploration of AI's rich history and milestones.
That book delved into the origins of machine learning, deep
learning, natural language processing (NLP), and large language
models (LLMs), and the rise of ChatGPT. It also examined AI
innovations by tech giants and startups, alongside diverse AI
business models that have reshaped industries.

This book, builds on that foundation. While the earlier book
focused on AI's historical evolution, this one delves deeper into its
technical intricacies, tailored specifically for IT professionals. From
foundational concepts to advanced applications.

For readers familiar with earlier work, this book serves as a deep
dive. For newcomers, it provides everything you need to embark
on your AI journey. Together, these books offer a holistic
understanding of AI—from its origins to its most cutting-edge
applications—empowering you to navigate and leverage the rapidly
evolving landscape of artificial intelligence.

Foreword

In a world driven by rapid technological advancements, artificial intelligence (AI) stands at the forefront of innovation, reshaping industries and redefining roles across the IT landscape. For IT professionals, keeping pace with these transformative changes is not just a necessity—it's an opportunity to future-proof careers and drive meaningful impact in their organizations.

In the fast-paced IT world, staying relevant requires more than just expertise in a specific domain—it demands a broader understanding of emerging technologies like AI. Artificial intelligence is no longer a niche field; it is transforming the way we approach problem-solving, automation, and innovation.

Authored by Mohammed Yousef Shaik, an AI entrepreneur and IT professional with over 18 years of experience, this book is thoughtfully designed for the IT community. A passionate advocate for knowledge sharing, the author recognizes that while IT professionals often excel in their specialized domains and remain deeply engaged in ongoing projects, this focus can limit opportunities to explore emerging technologies in depth. This book addresses that gap by introducing foundational AI concepts, delving into technical intricacies, exploring practical applications, and concluding with career pathways specifically tailored to IT roles.

By the end of this book, readers will gain a solid understanding, comprehensive awareness, and technical insights into the latest AI technologies, providing a robust foundation for further exploration and mastery.

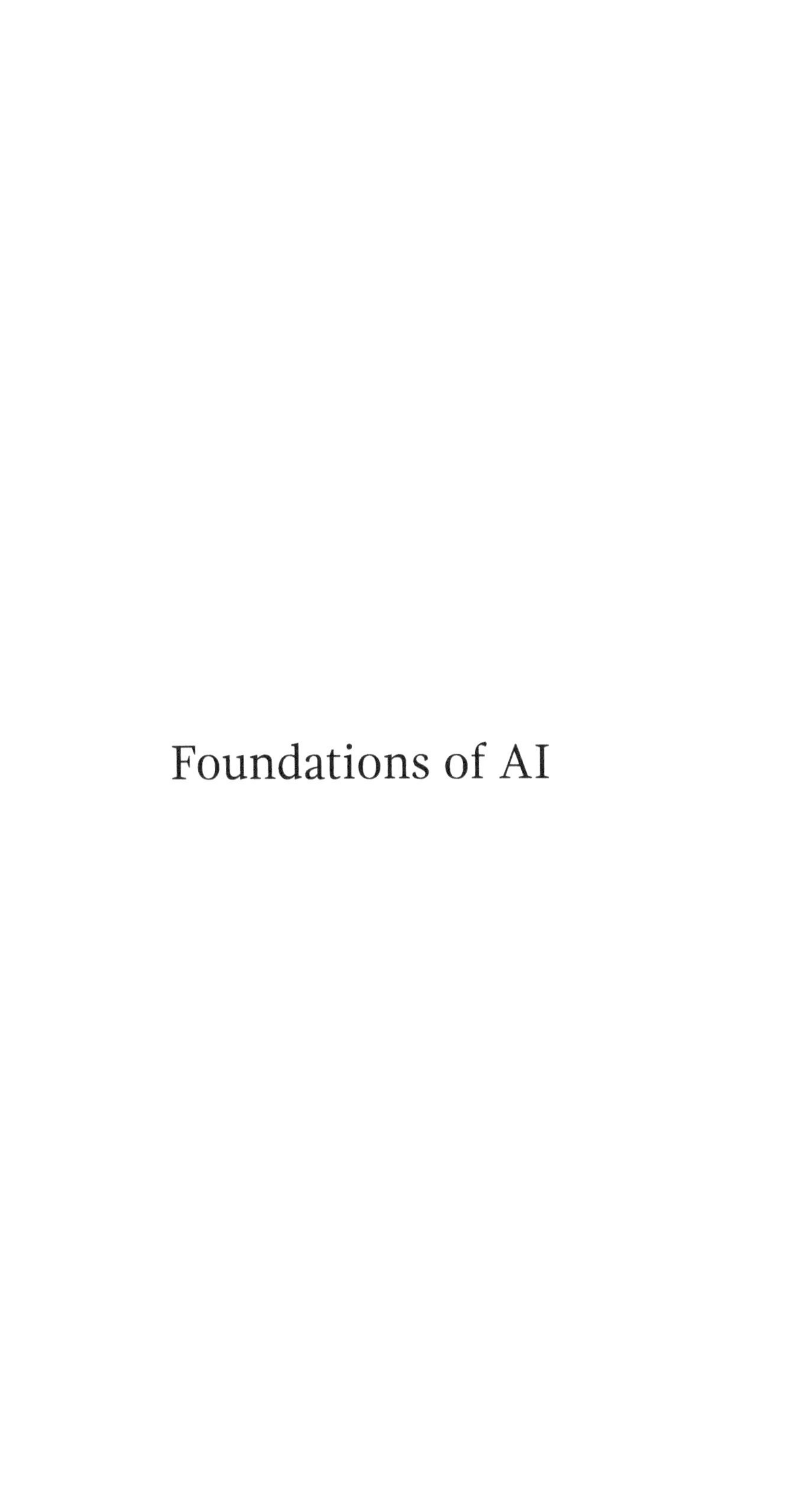

Foundations of AI

CHAPTER ONE

Transformational Landscape of AI

AI has become a necessity for modern enterprises. It is not just a buzzword but a technological revolution, reshaping industries, redefining roles, and unlocking unprecedented opportunities. From automating processes to enhancing decision-making, AI's transformative potential spans every domain, driving innovation and efficiency. As organizations embrace AI, it becomes the cornerstone for staying competitive in a rapidly evolving times.

An AI-Generated Illustration of Tech MNC

AI's Strategic Role in Modern Enterprises

Artificial Intelligence (AI) is rapidly becoming a cornerstone of modern enterprises, driving innovation, streamlining operations, and enabling new business opportunities. Beyond its role in efficiency and personalization, several critical factors are accelerating AI adoption across industries:

- **Competitive Advantage:** AI empowers businesses to innovate rapidly, offering unique products and services that differentiate them in the marketplace. By leveraging AI for continuous improvement, organizations can respond proactively to evolving market demands.
- **Cost Reduction:** By automating complex and resource-intensive processes, AI significantly reduces operational costs.
- **Enhanced Research and Development (R&D):** AI accelerates R&D efforts by analyzing vast datasets, identifying trends, and predicting outcomes. This capability shortens product development cycles and fosters innovation, enabling companies to stay competitive in dynamic markets.
- **Talent Augmentation:** AI enhances human capabilities by automating routine tasks and equipping employees with advanced tools. This allows professionals to focus on strategic and creative initiatives, boosting productivity and job satisfaction.
- **Market Expansion:** AI helps businesses identify untapped markets and customer segments.

AI is no longer optional for corporations—it's a necessity. In today's fast-paced world, businesses are already adopting AI to innovate, meet client demands, enhance internal growth, boost employee productivity, and unlock new profitability avenues.

Technological Innovations Fueling AI

- **Custom AI Hardware:** Specialized hardware is revolutionizing the way AI models are trained and deployed. Chips like NVIDIA's Tensor Core GPUs, Apple's Neural Engine, and Google's TPU (Tensor Processing Unit) offer unparalleled computational efficiency. These advancements are critical for powering complex tasks such as real-time language translation, generative AI applications, and autonomous systems.
- **Open-Source Ecosystems:** The proliferation of open-source tools like TensorFlow, PyTorch, and Hugging Face is democratizing AI development. These frameworks allow developers to leverage pre-built algorithms, collaborate globally, and innovate rapidly without starting from scratch. Open-source models, like Stable Diffusion and Bloom, have further enabled AI to flourish across creative and analytical domains.
- **Generative AI Models:** Generative AI is transforming industries by enabling creative automation. Tools such as GPT-4, DALL·E, and MidJourney are empowering businesses to produce realistic images, compelling text, and unique art at scale. These technologies enhance product design, marketing campaigns, and personalized client experiences.
- **Edge AI:** Edge computing brings AI closer to the source of data generation, such as IoT devices, reducing latency and enhancing real-time decision-making. AI-enabled devices like autonomous drones, smart cameras, and wearable health monitors utilize edge computing to deliver instant results in critical scenarios
- **Synthetic Data Generation:** The ability to create realistic, artificial datasets using tools like NVIDIA Omniverse and Gretel.ai has addressed data scarcity issues.

By leveraging advancements in hardware, open-source tools, generative AI, and edge computing, businesses can harness AI to unlock unprecedented efficiency, creativity, and scalability

AI's Influence on the Workforce

Artificial Intelligence (AI) is profoundly transforming the IT workforce, influencing job roles, skill requirements, and organizational structures. Key impacts include

- **Automation of Routine Tasks:** AI automates repetitive tasks such as data entry and system monitoring, allowing IT professionals to focus on strategic initiatives. This shift enhances productivity and fosters innovation within organizations.
- **Integration of AI in Daily Operations:** A significant percentage of professionals are utilizing AI to enhance efficiency in both generic and specialized tasks. Generic tasks include drafting emails and managing schedules, while niche applications involve developers using AI to debug code, generate scripts, accelerating delivery timelines and reducing errors. Support analysts leverage AI-driven tools to access past resolutions and knowledge bases, enabling quicker and more accurate responses to customer queries. Additionally, managers and leadership utilize AI for advanced reporting and strategic insights, empowering them to make data-driven decisions and identify new business opportunities.
- **Impact on Employment Rates:** The AI boom has contributed to shifts in employment within the tech industry, with traditional roles declining and new opportunities emerging in AI.
- **Job Displacement Concerns:** The automation capabilities of AI have raised concerns about job displacement, particularly in roles susceptible to automation.
- **Demand for Upskilling and Reskilling:** As AI technologies evolve, there is an increased need for IT professionals to acquire AI skills to remain competitive.
- **Creation of New Job Roles:** The rise of AI has led to new positions like Prompt Engineer, Data Scientist, AI Product Manager, Natural Language Processing (NLP) Engineer & More.

AI's Impact on Software Development

- **Democratization of Coding:** AI tools are lowering the barrier to entry for programming, enabling individuals without formal coding backgrounds to develop software through natural language prompts. This democratization fosters innovation and allows for a more diverse range of contributors to software projects.
- **Code Generation and Assistance:** Tools like GitHub Copilot and Amazon CodeWhisperer utilize AI to provide code suggestions and autocompletion, expediting the coding process and reducing errors. These assistants are trained on extensive codebases, enabling them to convert natural language prompts into executable code across various programming languages.
- **Automation of Repetitive Tasks:** AI-powered tools automate mundane tasks such as code reviews, testing, and debugging, allowing developers to focus on more complex and creative aspects of development. This leads to faster development cycles and higher-quality software
- **Efficiency for Developers:** AI accelerates repetitive tasks like debugging, script generation, and documentation. Advanced features like AI-driven testing and pseudocode languages enhance productivity and reduce errors.
- **Enhanced Collaboration:** Tools like Copilot Chat enable interactive coding, offering explanations and suggestions within the development environment.
- **Defect Prediction:** AI-driven defect prediction employs machine learning algorithms to analyze historical data, such as code metrics, bug reports, user interactions, and test results. By identifying patterns, it predicts areas where new defects are likely to emerge, enabling developers to address potential issues proactively before they escalate into critical production problems.

AI's Impact on Software Testing

Artificial Intelligence (AI) is significantly transforming software testing by enhancing efficiency, accuracy, and coverage. AI has become an indispensable tool in modern testing practices.

- **Automated Test Case Generation:** AI utilizes Natural Language Processing (NLP) to analyze requirements and user stories, generating comprehensive test cases. This automation reduces human effort, ensures consistency, and expands test coverage for complex software systems.
- **Defect Prediction:** Testers leverage AI-driven predictions to prioritize high-risk areas, design targeted test cases, refine regression testing strategies, and continuously enhance test plans, ensuring comprehensive coverage and improved software reliability.
- **Self-Healing Test Automation Tools:** Tools like Testim, mabl, and Tricentis Tosca leverage AI to identify and automatically update test scripts when changes in the application's UI, workflows, or data structures are detected.
- **Low-Code Test Automation:** Katalon Studio is a versatile software testing platform designed for quality assurance engineers and testers to automate testing across web applications, mobile apps, and APIs. Its low-code, drag-and-drop interface makes it accessible to users with varying technical expertise, streamlining creation, execution of automated tests.
- **Integration with CI/CD Pipelines:** AI-driven tools are embedded within CI/CD workflows to adapt tests automatically during deployments, ensuring seamless integration with evolving codebases.
- **AI-Driven Performance Testing:** AI tools such as Neotys NeoLoad, Dynatrace, and Apica analyze system performance under varying conditions, identifying bottlenecks and predicting potential scalability issues

AI's Impact on Broader Tech Roles

Artificial Intelligence is revolutionizing a wide range of tech roles, driving innovation and enhancing efficiency.

- **Architects:** Enterprise architects and system architects use tools like Grammatech and Ardoq to analyze system requirements and propose optimal architecture designs, thereby reducing manual effort.
- **Project Management:** AI-driven tools like Microsoft Project AI and Planview empower project managers to streamline workflows and deliver projects with greater efficiency. A notable trend emerging in service-based IT companies involves incorporating AI-based pricing strategies in response to RFPs. If clients permit the use of AI, the proposed pricing reflects cost efficiencies achieved through automation. Conversely, if clients restrict the use of AI, the quotation follows standard pricing models, accommodating traditional workflows
- **Proactive Incident Management:** AI-driven tools such as PagerDuty and Moogsoft utilize machine learning to correlate incidents across systems, enabling faster root cause analysis and resolution. This minimizes downtime and ensures seamless user experiences.
- **Application and Infrastructure Monitoring:** AI-powered monitoring tools like Dynatrace and New Relic analyze logs, metrics, and system performance in real-time. They proactively detect anomalies, predict failures, and provide actionable feedback, ensuring uninterrupted service and improved uptime.
- **Business Analysts:** AI-powered analytics platforms like Tableau with AI capabilities and Microsoft Power BI's "Smart Narratives" feature enable BAs to process large datasets efficiently. These tools uncover patterns, trends, and anomalies, helping BAs make data-driven recommendations faster.

Ethics and Governance in AI

As organizations embrace AI, ethical considerations and governance frameworks are essential to ensure fairness, transparency, and accountability. Addressing these challenges is critical for building trust in AI systems. Few Key Ethical Concerns.

- **Algorithmic Bias:** Biased training data can lead to unfair outcomes, emphasizing the need for diverse datasets and regular audits.
- **Transparency:** Explainable AI models help stakeholders understand and trust AI decisions, ensuring regulatory compliance.
- **Data Privacy:** Adhering to global data protection laws, such as GDPR, is vital for safeguarding user information.

Preparing for the Future of AI: AI is not a single technology but a continuously evolving ecosystem of tools, frameworks, and methodologies. For IT professionals, gaining a solid understanding of AI's foundational concepts is the essential first step toward unlocking its potential. The upcoming chapters will provide an in-depth exploration of the technical mechanics behind AI.

CHAPTER TWO

INTRODUCTION TO AI TECHNOLOGIES

The story of AI began in the mid-20th century, sparked by the question, "Can machines think?" Visionaries like Alan Turing and John McCarthy saw potential for machines to replicate human thought, and with that came the birth of AI as a field of study.

What is Artificial Intelligence?

Artificial Intelligence (AI) refers to the simulation of human intelligence in machines programmed to think, reason, and learn. These intelligent systems are designed to perform tasks that typically require human cognitive functions such as problem-solving, decision-making, language understanding, and perception. At its core, AI aims to enable machines to perform tasks autonomously, adaptively, and intelligently.

Evolution of AI

- **Rule-Based Systems (1950s–1980s):** Early AI systems were based on explicit rules and logic. Expert systems like MYCIN and DENDRAL were programmed with vast rule sets to solve specific problems but lacked adaptability and scalability.

- **Introduction of Machine Learning (1990s):** The advent of machine learning shifted AI from rule-based logic to data-driven approaches. Systems started learning patterns from data, enabling applications like fraud detection and recommendation systems.
- **Deep Learning Revolution (2010s):** Inspired by the human brain, deep learning utilizes neural networks with multiple layers to analyze complex data. Breakthroughs in computational power and access to massive datasets propelled advancements in image recognition, natural language processing (NLP), and generative AI models.
- **Modern AI Era (2020s):** Today, AI systems like ChatGPT and DALL-E leverage large language models (LLMs) and generative AI to produce human-like text, images, and audio. The focus has shifted to ethical AI, scalability, and democratization of AI tools.

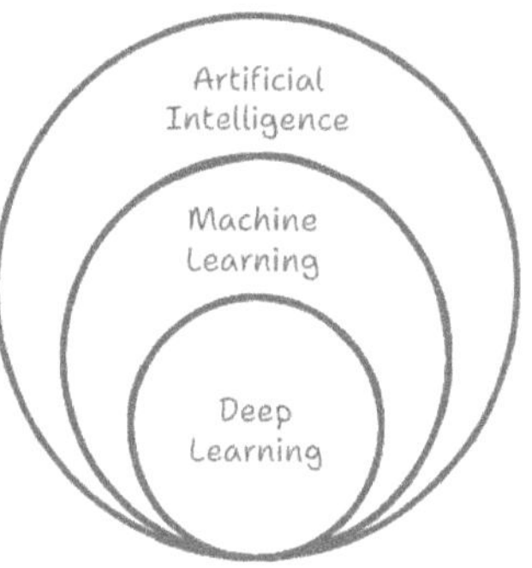

Feature engineering is the process of selecting, creating, or transforming raw data into meaningful features that can be used as inputs for machine learning models. This concept will be explored further in upcoming chapters.

Machine Learning (ML)

Machine learning is a subset of artificial intelligence that enables systems to learn patterns and make predictions from data without explicit programming. It uses algorithms to analyze data, identify patterns, and improve performance over time. Machine learning is widely applied in tasks like recommendation systems, fraud detection, and natural language processing.

- **Machine Learning Revolutionizes AI:** The 2000s marked a pivotal shift in AI with the rise of machine learning, which replaced traditional rule-based systems. Machine learning enabled computers to process data, adapt to new information, and make accurate predictions. This approach allowed AI to tackle complex problems across industries like healthcare, finance, and customer service, where analyzing vast amounts of data and deriving actionable insights became critical.
- **Data as the Foundation of AI:** The early 2000s witnessed an explosion of data due to the rapid expansion of digital connectivity. With the proliferation of mobile phones, computers, and the internet, the amount of data generated grew exponentially. This surge provided a rich foundation for machine learning algorithms, which depend on large datasets to identify patterns, improve prediction accuracy, and uncover hidden insights.
- **Smart Devices Amplify Data Growth:** The global adoption of smartphones and smart devices further fueled data generation. Social media interactions, online transactions, and data from IoT sensors created diverse and vast datasets. This influx of information not only empowered machine learning but also expanded AI's potential to analyze human behavior, predict trends, and improve decision-making across various domains.

The Core of Machine Learning

At its essence, machine learning empowers computers to enhance their performance on specific tasks through experience essentially, by learning from data. This approach depends on training algorithms on vast datasets, enabling systems to recognize patterns, make decisions, and generate predictions. The data explosion of the 2000s provided machine learning algorithms with the essential resources needed to create robust and adaptable models.

- **Supervised Learning:** Supervised learning involves training systems on labeled datasets—data with known outcomes—to predict future results. Common examples include spam email detection and credit scoring in financial applications.
- **Unsupervised Learning:** Unlike supervised learning, unsupervised learning works with unlabeled data to identify patterns, such as grouping customers by purchasing habits or segmenting images based on similar attributes.
- **Reinforcement Learning:** Although not as prominent in the 2000s, reinforcement learning (where systems learn by trial and error) set the stage for advanced applications in areas like robotics and gaming.

The Role of Big Data in Machine Learning Rise

Big Data refers to the massive volume of structured and unstructured data generated every second from various sources, such as social media, IoT devices, and online transactions. It involves analyzing and processing this data to uncover valuable insights, drive decision-making, and solve complex problems. Big Data has become a cornerstone of modern innovation, fueling advancements in artificial intelligence, predictive analytics, and personalized experiences.

An AI-Generated Illustration of ML & BigData

The image humorously illustrates the process of managing and analyzing vast amounts of information, highlighting the critical role of data processing in the world of artificial intelligence

The rise of big data was critical to machine learning's evolution. As internet usage skyrocketed, enormous amounts of information became available from sources like search engines, social media, e-commerce, and IoT devices. Companies began to recognize the immense value embedded in this data and invested heavily in storing and analyzing it.

- **Volume:** The sheer scale of data grew exponentially, creating vast opportunities for training more powerful machine learning models. Google and Amazon were among the early pioneers in leveraging massive datasets to improve their search algorithms and recommendation systems.
- **Variety:** Data sources became diverse, with information coming from text, images, audio, and video. This variety expanded the types of tasks machine learning could handle, from image recognition to natural language processing.

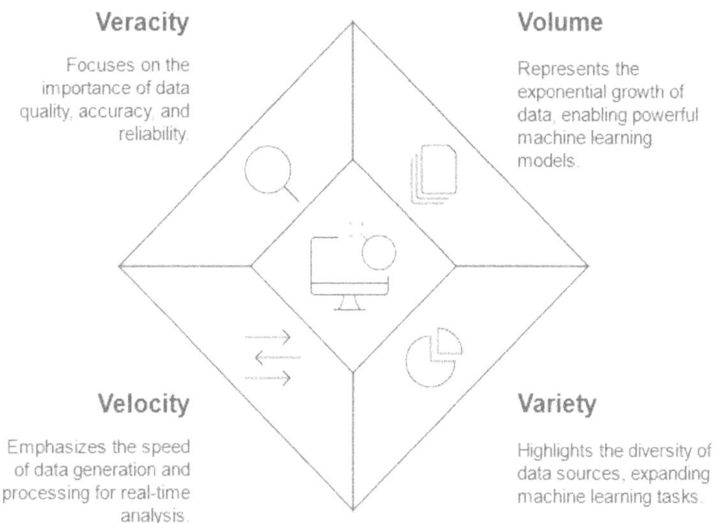

- **Velocity:** Data was generated and processed faster than ever, allowing real-time analysis. This capability was critical for applications like stock trading, where machine learning models needed to react quickly to market fluctuations.

- **Veracity:** As data volumes grew, ensuring data quality, accuracy, and reliability became crucial. Machine learning models are only as good as the data they're trained on, so addressing issues like data noise, inconsistencies, and biases became essential. Companies invested in data cleansing and validation processes, recognizing that accurate, high-quality data was critical to making reliable predictions and insights.

The rise of big data provided the essential fuel for machine learning's evolution. The combination of massive data volumes, diverse formats, and real-time processing enabled machine learning to become more accurate, adaptable, and impactful.

Technical Foundations : Algorithms and Models

In machine learning, algorithms are the core methods that define how data is processed, analyzed, and interpreted to make predictions or identify patterns. When algorithms are applied to specific data, they produce a 'model'—a structured representation of the insights extracted from that data. This model encapsulates patterns, trends, and relationships identified by the algorithm during its training process.

Essentially, a model is a mathematical construct that captures the underlying patterns in the data, enabling it to make predictions or decisions based on new, unseen data. For example, a model trained to recognize spam emails learns patterns from labeled emails, such as common keywords or sender behaviors. Once trained, the model can evaluate new emails and classify them accurately, applying the learned patterns without needing explicit rules for every scenario.

- **Decision Trees:** These were used for classification and regression tasks, breaking down complex decision-making processes into simpler, tree-like structures.

- **Support Vector Machines (SVMs):** SVMs became popular for classification tasks, especially in applications like image recognition.
- **Neural Networks:** Though still relatively simple, neural networks began to gain traction, with algorithms like backpropagation making training more effective.
- **K-Means Clustering:** Widely used for unsupervised learning, K-means clustering grouped data points based on similarity, helping with tasks like customer segmentation.

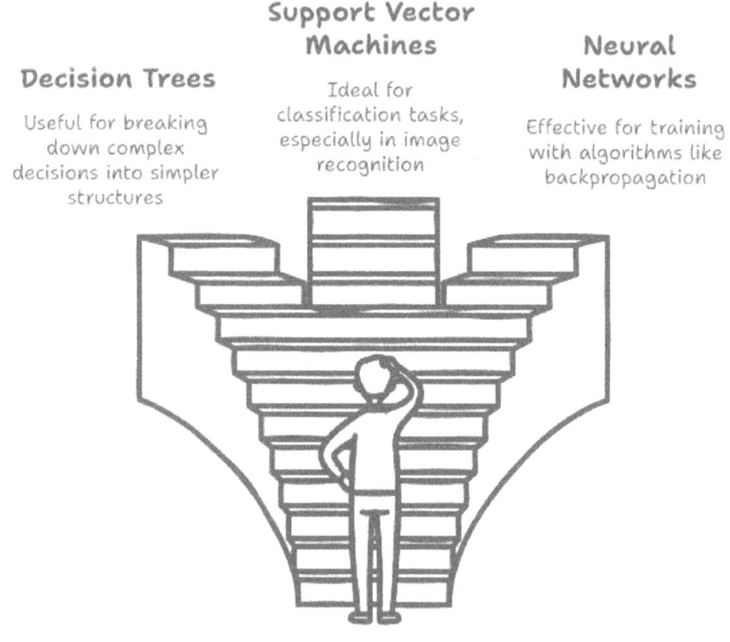

Machine Learning Techniques

These foundational algorithms and models laid the groundwork for machine learning's evolution, enabling systems to recognize patterns and make predictions in increasingly complex tasks.

Tech Stack For Building ML - Algorithms and Models

To develop and deploy machine learning (ML) solutions in 2024, a wide range of programming languages, frameworks, and tools are actively utilized to design, build, and optimize models for diverse real-world applications.

- **Python:** Python remains the most widely used language for machine learning and AI development. Its robust ecosystem includes frameworks like TensorFlow, PyTorch, and Scikit-learn for model development, alongside NumPy and Pandas for data preprocessing. With its extensive community support and integration capabilities, Python dominates both research and production environments
- **R:** R continues to be favored for statistical modeling, data visualization, and specific applications like epidemiology and bioinformatics. Popular libraries like tidyverse, caret, and ggplot2 ensure its utility for machine learning tasks such as exploratory data analysis and predictive modeling.
- **Java:** Java remains relevant in large-scale enterprise applications, particularly for integrating machine learning models into existing systems. Frameworks like DL4J (Deep Learning for Java) and Weka provide reliable options for implementing and testing algorithms in production pipelines.
- **Julia:** Julia has gained significant traction in ML and AI for its speed and high-performance capabilities, rivaling C++ in computational efficiency while being easier to use. Libraries like Flux and MLJ make Julia an excellent choice for scalable machine learning applications, particularly in fields like finance and scientific computing.
- **MATLAB:** is still a top choice in academia and engineering fields. used for prototyping, algorithm testing, and numerical analysis.
- **C++:** For performance-intensive domains like computer vision, robotics, and gaming.

Supporting Infrastructure For Machine Learning

In 2024, machine learning continues to thrive, supported by advanced infrastructure that enables deployment, scalability, and efficient management.

- **Cloud Computing Services:** Fully managed cloud platforms like AWS, Google Cloud, and Microsoft Azure have become the backbone of machine learning infrastructure. These platforms provide scalable solutions for training, deploying, and managing ML models while offering integrations with various AI and ML services.
- **GPUs and TPUs:** GPUs from NVIDIA and TPUs (Tensor Processing Units) from Google remain at the forefront of hardware accelerators. They provide unparalleled speed for training large-scale ML models and powering tasks ranging from generative AI to advanced computer vision applications.
- **Data Storage and Management:** Modern data storage solutions like Amazon S3, Azure Data Lake, and Snowflake ensure efficient handling of structured, semi-structured, and unstructured data. These systems integrate seamlessly with analytics pipelines and ML workflows to enhance accessibility and scalability.
- **Containerization and Orchestration:** Tools like Docker and Kubernetes have become indispensable for creating isolated, scalable environments. They enable the seamless deployment and orchestration of machine learning applications across diverse infrastructures, improving flexibility and resource efficiency.
- **Data Pipelines and ETL (Extract, Transform, Load):** Advanced tools like Apache Airflow, Apache Beam, and AWS Glue automate the data preparation process. Streamlining data extraction, transformation, and loading, ensuring datasets are optimized for ML model training and operational use.

Real-World Machine Learning Applications

Machine learning remains a cornerstone of technological advancement across industries, driving innovation in areas ranging from healthcare to marketing. Organizations increasingly rely on ML to build predictive models, streamline operations, and make informed decisions.

- **Finance:** Financial institutions use ML for fraud detection, credit risk assessment, and algorithmic trading. Modern ML systems analyze massive datasets in real time, identifying anomalies, predicting market trends with unparalleled accuracy.
- **Healthcare:** ML is transforming healthcare through AI-assisted diagnostics, medical imaging analysis, and disease risk prediction. In 2024, ML-powered tools are widely used for personalized treatment recommendations, remote patient monitoring, and outbreak prediction, enabling faster and more precise healthcare interventions.
- **Retail and Marketing:** Retail giants like Amazon and Flipkart continue to use advanced recommendation systems powered by machine learning to deliver personalized shopping experiences. ML optimizes inventory management, forecasts demand with greater accuracy, and enhances customer engagement through predictive analytics and targeted marketing.
- **Transportation:** In the transportation sector, ML drives innovation in autonomous vehicles, real-time route optimization, and fleet management. Predictive maintenance systems powered by AI minimize downtime and reduce costs, while dynamic scheduling systems improve logistics efficiency.
- **Telecommunications:** Telecom companies deploy machine learning for 5G network optimization, predictive infrastructure maintenance, and customer experience automation. AI-powered solutions now proactively detect network issues, enabling faster resolutions and reducing service disruptions.

Deep Learning

In the early 2010s, while machine learning was effective for structured data, the growing need for AI systems to tackle complex tasks like image and speech recognition highlighted its limitations with unstructured data. This led researchers and tech giants to turn to a new approach: deep learning.

An AI-Generated Illustration of Deep Learning

Deep learning, a transformative subset of machine learning, is inspired by the structure and functioning of the human brain. It utilizes artificial neural networks—sophisticated computational systems designed to mimic how neurons in the brain transmit and process information. Like the brain, where neurons activate in intricate patterns to recognize and respond to stimuli, deep learning models rely on multiple layers of artificial "neurons" to analyze data, detect patterns, and make predictions.

Each layer in a deep neural network is designed to extract specific features from the input data, resembling how various regions of the human brain handle distinct sensory tasks. For instance, in image recognition, initial layers may identify basic elements such as edges and shapes, while deeper layers detect complex patterns like textures or objects. This hierarchical structure allows deep learning models to process raw, unstructured data step by step, refining their understanding at each stage.This layered approach remains foundational to advancements in AI, driving innovations across domains such as autonomous systems, natural language processing, and generative technologies.

Difference between Deep Learning & Machine Learning

Data Requirements: One of the primary distinctions between machine learning and deep learning lies in the scale of data required. Machine learning can perform well with smaller datasets by leveraging feature engineering to extract meaningful patterns. Deep learning, however, thrives on vast amounts of data, as it relies on neural networks to identify intricate patterns and relationships. In 2024, with data availability growing exponentially, deep learning has become increasingly viable for solving complex problems.

Feature Engineering: In traditional machine learning, feature engineering is often manual and requires domain expertise to select and transform relevant data attributes. This process can be time-intensive and subjective. Deep learning, by contrast, automates feature extraction, analyzing raw data through its layered neural networks. This eliminates the need for manual feature selection, making it especially effective for tasks like image and speech recognition, where the relationships between features are complex and non-linear.

Complexity and Interpretability: Deep learning models, particularly those with many layers, are often considered "black boxes" due to their lack of interpretability. This opacity can pose challenges in critical domains like healthcare, where understanding decision-making processes is vital. Conversely, machine learning models are generally more transparent, offering straightforward relationships between input features and predictions. While efforts in 2024 continuc to improve deep learning explainability, traditional machine learning retains an edge in scenarios demanding clarity and accountability.

Accuracy and Versatility: Deep learning outperforms machine learning in tasks involving unstructured data such as images, audio, and text, achieving breakthroughs in natural language processing, computer vision, and autonomous systems. However, for simpler tasks or limited datasets, machine learning remains a better choice due to its lower computational overhead and efficiency in handling structured data. The balance between task complexity and data availability remains a key consideration in 2024.

Computational Power: Deep learning requires significant computational resources, often relying on GPUs, TPUs, or distributed cloud-based architectures to train models efficiently. Machine learning, on the other hand, is less resource-intensive and can be executed on standard hardware, making it more suitable for smaller-scale projects or environments with limited infrastructure. The accessibility of cloud services in 2024 has lowered entry barriers for deep learning but continues to favor machine learning in constrained settings.

Machine Learning Applications: Machine learning excels in applications requiring structured data and simpler predictive tasks. Typical use cases include fraud detection, customer segmentation, and predictive maintenance. Its efficiency and straightforward deployment make it indispensable for businesses looking to optimize operations with minimal computational demands.

Deep Learning Applications: Deep learning is the go-to solution for complex and unstructured data challenges. Its ability to process massive datasets with high accuracy has solidified its role in pushing the boundaries of AI applications.

Tech Stack for Building Deep Learning Models

- **Keras:** As a high-level API integrated with TensorFlow, Keras simplifies deep learning development with its intuitive interface and modular design. Its prebuilt layers and visualization tools for monitoring training processes make it a preferred choice for both prototyping and production-ready models.
- **Julia:** With its high-performance capabilities and JIT compilation, Julia is increasingly used for deep learning. Libraries like Flux and Metalhead support scalable deep learning projects, particularly in fields requiring speed and computational efficiency, such as scientific simulations and financial modeling.
- **Similar to Machine Learning:** Deep Learning also relies on tools and languages like Python, TensorFlow, PyTorch, R, MATLAB, and C++. Frameworks like TensorFlow and PyTorch, however, are specifically optimized for building and training neural network models, making them indispensable for deep learning tasks.

Algorithms and Models in Deep Learning

Deep learning algorithms power AI by analyzing large datasets to find patterns and make predictions. They create models that mimic the human brain, using layers of artificial neurons to process raw data step by step. For example, in speech recognition, early layers detect sounds, while deeper layers identify words and context. This helps deep learning excel at tasks involving complex, unstructured data.

In deep learning, an algorithm refers to the process or method used to train a neural network. A model is the trained result of this proccss, capablc of making prcdictions or pcrforming spccific tasks. Below are a few examples of algorithms and models.

- **Convolutional Neural Networks (CNNs):** Used extensively in computer vision, CNNs power applications such as facial recognition, medical image analysis, and autonomous vehicles by capturing spatial hierarchies within visual data.
- **Recurrent Neural Networks (RNNs):** These models are ideal for processing sequential data, making them indispensable in time-series forecasting, speech recognition, and machine translation.
- **Transformers:** Leveraging self-attention mechanisms, transformers are now foundational in natural language processing and computer vision. They power models like GPT for text generation and BERT for sentiment analysis.
- **Autoencoders:** Common in unsupervised learning, they perform tasks like anomaly detection, noise reduction, dimensionality reduction by learning compact representations of input data.
- **Generative Adversarial Networks (GANs):** GANs revolutionized synthetic data generation, creating realistic images, videos, music through interplay of two neural networks, one generating data and the other evaluating authenticity.

Real-World Deep Learning Applications

Deep learning continues to revolutionize industries, transforming workflows and driving innovation across fields like healthcare, automotive, retail, finance, entertainment, education, and beyond.

- **Healthcare:** Advanced deep learning models enhance medical imaging and diagnostics, detecting conditions like cancer, heart disease, and neurological disorders with unmatched accuracy. These advancements enable earlier detection, personalized treatment planning, and improved patient outcomes.
- **Automotive:** Deep learning drives the progress of autonomous vehicles by interpreting complex sensor data, recognizing objects and road conditions, and making critical driving decisions. This technology is integral to advancing self-driving cars and improving traffic safety systems.
- **Retail and E-commerce:** Industry giants like Amazon utilize deep learning for sophisticated recommendation engines, delivering hyper-personalized shopping experiences by analyzing purchase patterns and browsing behavior. This enhances customer satisfaction and boosts sales conversions.
- **Finance:** Fraud detection systems powered by deep learning analyze transactional data in real time, identifying unusual activities and mitigating risks. Algorithmic trading also benefits from deep learning, optimizing trading strategies and ensuring faster responses to market fluctuations.
- **Entertainment and Media:** Deep learning underpins cutting-edge technologies like voice assistants (e.g., Siri, Alexa) and content personalization algorithms for streaming platforms. These systems provide intuitive user interactions and tailor content to individual preferences.

Natural Language Processing (NLP)

Natural Language Processing (NLP) is a branch of artificial intelligence that empowers computers to understand, interpret, and generate human language. This transformative technology enables machines to process and analyze text and speech, driving applications such as language translation, voice assistants, and advanced text analytics.

An AI-Generated Illustration of Natural Language Processing (NLP)

Technical Foundations: Algorithms, Models and Techniques in NLP

In Natural Language Processing (NLP), algorithms and models form the backbone of enabling machines to understand, interpret, and generate human language. By applying these algorithms to text or speech, systems produce "models"—structured frameworks capable of identifying linguistic patterns, extracting meaning, and generating contextually relevant responses. These models encapsulate the syntax, semantics, and pragmatics of language, allowing computers to process human communication effectively.

NLP models integrate statistical methods with linguistic rules to handle unstructured language data for tasks like language translation, text summarization, and sentiment analysis. For example, a model trained on labeled datasets for sentiment analysis learns patterns in text, such as keywords or contextual phrases, to classify sentiment as positive, negative, or neutral. Once trained, the model can analyze new text and provide accurate predictions without requiring explicit rules for each scenario.

- **Tokenization:** This foundational step divides text into smaller units like words, subwords, or sentences, forming the building blocks for further analysis in tasks like language modeling and machine translation.
- **Transformers:** These advanced models, powered by attention mechanisms, revolutionized NLP by processing entire sequences of text while capturing long-range dependencies and context. Popular frameworks like GPT and BERT leverage transformers to deliver state-of-the-art performance in various NLP tasks.
- **Recurrent Neural Networks (RNNs):** Initially prominent for sequential text data, RNNs and their variants, like LSTMs (Long Short-Term Memory networks), process language by retaining information across sequences, making them suitable for speech-to-text and machine translation.

- **Named Entity Recognition (NER):** NER is vital for extracting structured information from text. pre-trained transformer models like RoBERTa and fine-tuned BERT have improved NER's accuracy, especially in fields like healthcare and finance. Tools like spaCy now integrate these advanced models, making NER systems more accurate and adaptable.
- **Semantic Parsing:** Semantic parsing has advanced significantly, incorporating pre-trained language models to convert natural language inputs into structured data with higher precision. It's now widely used in question-answering systems, robotic process automation (RPA), and intelligent customer support systems, aligning closely with conversational AI platforms.
- **Pre-trained Language Models:** Large pre-trained models like GPT-4 and LLaMA have become central to NLP. These models serve as general-purpose backbones, fine-tuned for specific tasks, offering state-of-the-art performance in multiple domains.
- **Zero-shot and Few-shot Learning:** Modern NLP systems leverage transfer learning to perform tasks with minimal labeled data. These techniques enable models like OpenAI's GPT or Google's T5 to generalize effectively without task-specific training.
- **Speech-to-Text and Text-to-Speech (STT and TTS):** NLP's integration with deep learning has greatly improved these technologies, making voice assistants like Alexa and Google Assistant more accurate and human-like in their interactions.
- **Sentiment Analysis:** While traditionally a separate task, sentiment analysis now incorporates fine-tuned transformer-based models to assess nuanced emotions, helping businesses with real-time customer feedback and social media monitoring.

These advancements have further refined NLP's capabilities, enabling it to tackle increasingly complex language-based tasks and align closely with human needs.

Technology Stack for Building NLP Algorithms and Models

To develop and deploy Natural Language Processing (NLP) solutions, a variety of programming languages, frameworks, and tools have evolved to process and analyze human language effectively, reflecting advancements up to 2024.

- Python: Python continued to dominate NLP due to its extensive ecosystem. Libraries like NLTK (pioneering in the early 2000s) and spaCy (launched in 2015) remained widely used for traditional NLP tasks. By 2024, Hugging Face's Transformers library became the cornerstone for leveraging pre-trained models such as BERT, GPT, and T5, simplifying fine-tuning for applications like text summarization, machine translation, and sentiment analysis.
- R: R maintained relevance in text mining and statistical linguistics, favored by researchers for its analytical capabilities. Packages like tm and quanteda enabled efficient text preprocessing and visualization, while RMarkdown facilitated the integration of NLP insights into reproducible reports.
- Java: Java remained a robust choice for enterprise NLP systems. Frameworks like Apache OpenNLP and Stanford CoreNLP provided scalable solutions for tasks like named entity recognition, syntactic parsing, and sentiment analysis. Its widespread use in production systems highlighted its reliability and strong community support.
- Rust and Julia: By 2024, Rust and Julia gained popularity for computationally intensive NLP tasks requiring low latency. Rust's Oxen library enabled efficient text processing pipelines, while Julia's TextAnalysis.jl provided high-performance tools for large-scale text analytics and natural language understanding.
- And C++ & MATLAB remained critical for performance-intensive applications.

Real-World NLP Applications

Customer support chatbots have evolved to leverage advanced NLP and generative AI, offering conversational experiences that feel human-like. These chatbots can understand context, sentiment, and intent, enabling them to handle complex inquiries.

An AI-Generated Illustration of Chatbot

They can resolve customer issues, upsell products, and even predict user needs, offering businesses an intelligent, cost-effective way to enhance customer engagement and satisfaction.

Email Filtering & Spam Detection

Email filtering systems leverage advanced NLP models like transformers, using contextual understanding to classify emails as spam or legitimate.

An AI-Generated Illustration Email Filtering & Spam Detection

Modern NLP systems analyze email content, metadata, and user behavior to detect spam and phishing attempts with high reliability. Email providers leverage AI models like BERT-based classifiers and transformers to block unwanted and harmful emails.

The scope of AI is far broader than what was covered in this chapter. Additional AI technologies are shaping the future in profound ways.

- **Computer Vision:** Used in facial recognition, autonomous vehicles, and medical imaging.
- **Robotics:** Integrating AI for automation in industries like manufacturing, healthcare, and logistics.
- **Generative AI:** Creating new content, such as images, videos, and music, using transformer-based models like DALL-E and Stable Diffusion.
- **Reinforcement Learning:** Critical for advancements in autonomous systems and gaming.
- **Edge AI:** Bringing AI computations closer to devices for faster processing and real-time decision-making.
- **AI Agents:** Performing complex tasks such as automating workflows, booking appointments, and managing communications.

These emerging technologies promise to expand AI's potential even further, ensuring its integration into every facet of daily life.

CHAPTER THREE

HOW MACHINES LEARN

Machines learn through processes that allow them to recognize patterns, make decisions, and adapt based on data. This chapter will break down these processes into easy-to-understand concepts, covering learning paradigms, neural networks, and how we evaluate the effectiveness of machine learning models. By the end, you'll have a practical understanding of how machines learn and how we ensure their learning leads to meaningful results.

Learning Paradigms

Machine learning (ML) relies on three main learning paradigms. Think of these paradigms as different ways of teaching a machine based on the kind of information we have.

Supervised Learning: Teaching with Examples

In supervised learning, we provide the machine with labeled examples. For every input, we tell the machine what the correct output should be. Over time, the machine learns the relationship between inputs and outputs.

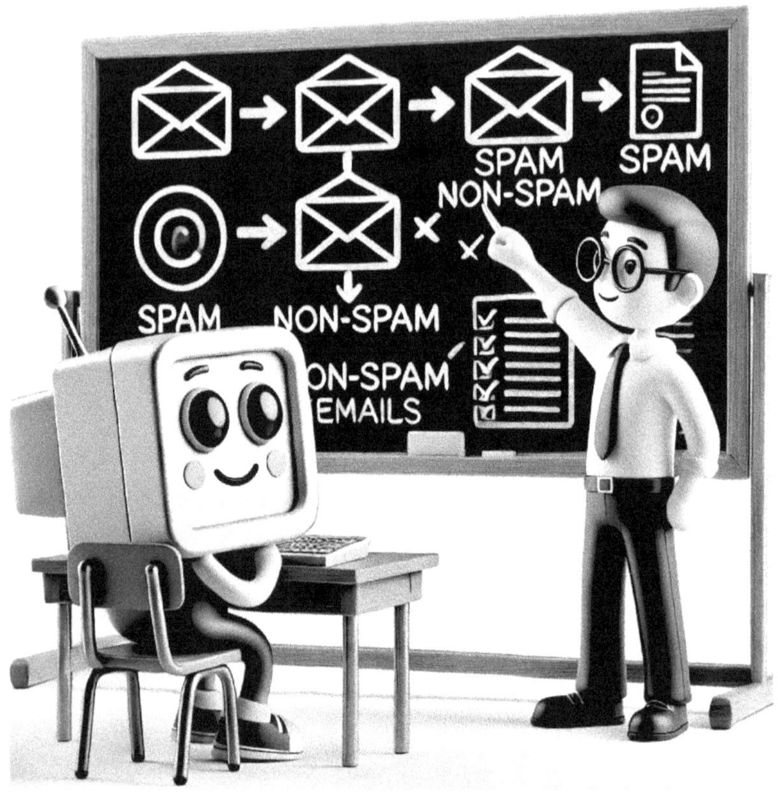

An AI-Generated Illustration of Supervised Learning

Example: Training a Spam Filter

Let's dive deeper into how a spam filter is trained and works, breaking it down into practical, easy-to-understand steps

Step 1: Collecting and Preparing Data

To train a spam filter, we first need a dataset containing emails that have already been labeled as "Spam" or "Not Spam". This dataset acts as the machine's teacher, helping it learn to differentiate between the two categories.

Input: The email's content, such as subject lines, body text, Example - Subject: "Congratulations! You've won $1,000! - Body: "Click here to claim your prize now!"

Output: A label that identifies whether the email is spam or not. Example: The email above would be labeled as "Spam."

	Email Content	Label
0	Win a free vacation! Click here.	Spam
1	Meeting scheduled for Monday at 10 AM.	Not Spam
2	Low-interest loan available, apply now!	Spam
3	Your bank statement is ready.	Not Spam
4	Exclusive offer: Buy 1 Get 1 Free!	Spam
5	Can we reschedule our appointment to Wednesday?	Not Spam
6	Urgent: Update your account details immediately.	Spam
7	Your package has been shipped and is on its way.	Not Spam
8	You have won a lottery! Claim now.	Spam
9	Reminder: Project deadline is tomorrow at noon.	Not Spam

Sample Dataset

Step 2: Feature Extraction

Machines can't understand raw text the way humans do, so we need to convert the email content into a format they can process—numerical features.

- **Tokenization:** Break the email into individual words or phrases (called tokens). Example: "You've won $1,000!" → ["You've", "won", "$1,000"]

- **Frequency Count:** Measure how often certain words appear in spam vs. non-spam emails. Example: Words like "win," "free," and "prize" may appear frequently in spam emails, while "meeting" and "schedule" appear more in legitimate emails.
- **Other Features:** Presence of certain symbols (e.g., "$", "!!!").Unusual sender addresses (e.g., "lottery@dcrr.com") Embedded links or attachments.

This process transforms the email into a feature vector—a list of numbers representing the presence or frequency of words and patterns.

	Word	Email 1	Email 2
0	Win	1	0
1	Free	1	0
2	Meeting	0	1
3	Loan	0	0
4	...	...	...

Word Frequency Dataset

Step 3: Training the Model

Once your data is ready, you train the model using an algorithm. This step helps the model learn patterns in the data so it can classify emails (or any other input) correctly.

What Happens During Training?
The algorithm looks at the features in the training data (e.g., words like "win" or "free") and learns which ones are most likely associated with spam or not spam.

Example: If the word "win" appears, the model may learn that there's an 80% chance the email is spam. If the word "meeting" appears, it might learn that there's only a 10% chance the email is spam.

These "chances" are weights assigned to features. The model adjusts these weights as it processes more data, becoming smarter and more accurate

Algorithm for Spam Filtering: A common choice is the Naïve Bayes algorithm, which calculates the likelihood of an email being spam based on the features (e.g., word frequencies). This algorithm is simple, fast, and effective for text classification tasks like spam detection.

Example: If words like "win" and "free" appear together, there's a high probability the email is spam. If the email contains words like "meeting" and "schedule," it's likely not spam.

The model assigns weights to each word or feature based on its importance. For instance:"Win" might have a weight of 0.8 (strong spam indicator)."Meeting" might have a weight of 0.1 (not likely spam).The weights are adjusted as the model processes more data, improving its accuracy.

How to Choose the Right Algorithm for a Task
The choice of algorithm depends on the problem you're trying to solve and the type of data you have. You will find them in Libraries like scikit-learn in Python, OpenAI Gym, Stable Baselines, TensorFlow, PyTorch.

In this case we choose Naïve Bayes algorithm, as its great for text classification (spam detection, sentiment analysis).

Step 4: Making Predictions

After training, the model is ready to classify new, unseen emails. Here's how it works in practice:

Input: A new email arrives
Subject: "Get your free credit card now!"
Body: "Limited-time offer. Apply today to save big!"

Feature Extraction: Email is tokenized, features are extracted:
Words: ["free", "credit", "card", "save", "big"].
Frequency and patterns are analyzed.

Prediction:
The model calculates the likelihood of the email being spam vs. not spam. Based on its training, it identifies "free" and "limited-time offer" as strong spam indicators.

Result: The model predicts that this email is spam.

Step 5: Evaluating and Improving the Model

To ensure the spam filter performs well, we test it on a separate dataset (testing data) that the model hasn't seen before. Some metrics used

- **Accuracy:** The percentage of emails correctly classified as spam or not spam.
- **Precision:** Of all emails marked as spam, how many were actually spam?
- **Recall:** Of all the actual spam emails, how many did the filter catch?
- **Continuous Learning:** The spam filter needs to evolve as spam tactics change. New training data is added periodically to improve its detection capabilities.

Unsupervised Learning

Unsupervised learning is a type of machine learning where the model learns from unlabeled data. Unlike supervised learning, there are no predefined outputs. The goal is to identify hidden patterns, structures, or groupings in the data.

It's like giving the machine a puzzle without instructions and letting it figure out how to piece things together.

An AI-Generated Illustration of Unsupervised Learning

Real-World Example: Movie Recommendation System

Imagine a streaming service (like Netflix) that wants to recommend movies to users without knowing their specific preferences or past viewing habits. Using unsupervised learning, the system can group users into categories and suggest movies based on these patterns.

Step 1: Data Collection

Dataset: The streaming service collects information such as

- Age of the viewer.
- Genres liked (e.g., action, comedy, drama).
- Average viewing time.
- Ratings given to movies.
- Interaction data (e.g., what they clicked on or ignored).

	Viewer ID	Age	Genres Watched	Avg Hrs
0	V001	20	Action, Comedy	2.5
1	V002	35	Drama, Thriller	4.0
2	V003	50	Romance, Drama	3.5
3	V004	25	Comedy, Action	1.8

Viewers Data

Step 2: Feature Representation

The system converts qualitative data into numerical formats for analysis. For example:

- Genres are encoded as binary values
- Action = 1 if the viewer watches action movies; otherwise, 0.
- Comedy = 1 if the viewer watches comedy; otherwise, 0.
- Viewing times and age are directly represented as numerical values.

Viewer ID	Age	Action	Comedy	Drama	Thriller	Romance	Viewing Time (hrs)
V001	20	1	1	0	0	0	2.5
V002	35	0	0	1	1	0	4.0
V003	50	0	0	1	0	1	3.5
V004	25	1	1	0	0	0	1.8

Encoding table example

Step 3: Applying Clustering Algorithms

The system applies unsupervised learning algorithms, to group viewers based on their preferences and behavior. The process as follows

- **Initial Clusters:** The algorithm begins by placing cluster centers randomly within the dataset's feature space (e.g., age, genres watched, viewing time). Each viewer's data point is assigned to the cluster center closest to them based on a mathematical distance metric, such as Euclidean distance. For example: Viewer V001 (young, action-comedy fan) may initially be assigned to Cluster 1. Viewer V003 (older, romance-drama fan) may be assigned to Cluster 2.
- **Cluster Refinement:** After the initial assignment, the algorithm calculates the "mean" position of all viewers in each cluster. This becomes the new cluster center. Viewers are reassigned to the

cluster whose center is now closest to them after recalibration. This process of recalculating cluster centers and reassigning viewers is repeated until the clusters stabilize (i.e., no more changes in assignments).

Step 4: Identifying Patterns

The algorithm analyzes the formed clusters to discover patterns:

- **Cluster 1 - Young Action-Comedy Lovers: Characteristics:** Viewers aged 18-30 with a preference for action and comedy. Example: V001 and V004 belong to this cluster.
- **Cluster 2 - Mature Drama Enthusiasts: Characteristics:** Viewers aged 35-50 who prefer drama and thriller genres. Example: V002 and V003 are grouped here.
- **Cluster 3 - Heavy Watchers: Characteristics:** Viewers with an average viewing time >3.5 hours, indicating higher engagement.

Step 5: Insights and Recommendations

After identifying clusters, the system uses these patterns to personalize recommendations.

- **For Cluster 1 (Young Action-Comedy Lovers):** Suggest trending action movies like "Fast & Furious" or popular sitcoms like "Friends."
- **For Cluster 2 (Mature Drama Enthusiasts):** Suggest critically acclaimed dramas like "The Crown" or thrillers like "Breaking Bad."
- **For Cluster 3 (Heavy Watchers):** Suggest longer, story-driven series like "The Witcher" or "Game of Thrones."

Disclaimer: All trademarks, Platform name, movie titles, and series names mentioned in this book are the property of their respective owners. These references are used for educational purposes only and do not imply endorsement or affiliation.

Watching a movie recommended by the system.

- **Dynamic Adjustments:** As new data (e.g., a new viewer or updated viewing history) enters the system, clusters can adapt dynamically. For instance, a viewer previously in Cluster 1 might shift to Cluster 2 if their preferences change.
- **Patterns Without Labels:** Unlike supervised learning, unsupervised learning doesn't require labeled data. It identifies natural groupings solely based on shared characteristics in the dataset.

By applying these techniques, the system ensures highly personalized recommendations for every user, enhancing engagement and viewer satisfaction.

Reinforcement Learning: Learning by Trial and Error

Reinforcement learning (RL) involves training an agent to interact with an environment by learning from feedback in the form of rewards and punishments. The agent's objective is to maximize cumulative rewards over time, refining its decisions through a balance of exploration (trying new actions) and exploitation (choosing the best-known action).

AI Robot - Learning to Walk

Goal: Train a robot to walk by rewarding stable steps and punishing falls.

Step 1: Define the Environment

The robot operates within an environment (e.g., a flat surface). This environment provides:

- **States:** Information about the robot's balance, position, and movement (e.g., upright, leaning, falling).
- **Actions:** Movements the robot can take (e.g., move left leg, right leg, adjust posture)

Rewards/Punishments:

- **Staying upright:** +10 points.
- **Taking a step forward:** +5 points.
- **Falling:** -20 points.

Step 2: Initialize the Agent

The robot starts with no knowledge of the environment. It initially explores randomly

- **State Representation:** The robot captures the current position, balance, and movement as numerical features.
- **Action Space:** Defines all possible movements (e.g., forward step, backward step, adjust tilt).
- **Reward Function:** Maps actions to rewards or penalties.

Step 3: Choose an RL Algorithm

Choosing the right Reinforcement Learning (RL) algorithm depends on the complexity of your task and the available data. RL algorithms can be found in Python libraries like OpenAI Gym,

Stable-Baselines3, TensorFlow, and PyTorch. Additionally, open-source RL projects with Q-Learning implementations are available on GitHub to explore.

For this use case, we will use the Q-Learning algorithm, a model-free reinforcement learning method that doesn't need prior knowledge of how actions lead to outcomes. Instead, it learns by trial and error, updating a Q-Table based on its experiences.

	State	Move Left Leg	Move Right Leg	Tilt Forward	Tilt Backward
0	Upright	10	8	5	-2
1	Leaning Left	-10	12	7	-5
2	Falling	-20	-20	-15	-15

Example Q-Table for a Walking Robot

Step 4: Training the Agent

This is how the robot learns step by step through trial and error:

- **Start with the Current Situation (State):** The robot observes its current state. For example, is it upright or leaning?
- **Decide What to Do (Choose an Action):** Explore - Try a random action (like moving the left leg) to discover new possibilities. Or Exploit - Choose the best-known action (based on the Q-Table) to get the highest reward.
- **Perform the Action:** The robot executes the chosen action, like tilting forward or moving its right leg.
- **Get Feedback (Reward or Punishment):** Reward - If the action helps robot stay upright, it earns +ve points (a reward). If the action makes the robot fall, it loses points (a punishment).
- **Update What It Knows (Q-Table):** The robot adjusts its Q-Table, which is like its memory. It improves its understanding of which actions lead to rewards.

How the Robot Updates Its Learning

The robot uses a simple formula.

$$Q(s,a) = Q(s,a) + \alpha\big(R + \gamma \cdot \max_a Q(s',a) - Q(s,a)\big)$$

Formula to adjust its Q-values:

- **Q(s, a):** The current understanding of how good the action is for the current state.
- **α (Learning Rate):** Controls how much the robot learns from new experiences. Small values make learning slow; large values make learning fast.
- **R (Reward):** The points the robot gets after taking the action.
- **γ (Discount Factor):** How much future rewards matter compared to immediate rewards.
- **max Q(s', a):** The best action the robot can take in the next state.

Step 5: Refining the Policy

The policy is a mapping from states to actions, derived from the Q-Table. As training progresses

- The robot refines its policy by consistently choosing actions with the highest Q-values
- Over time, the robot transitions from random exploration to optimized walking strategies

By the end of training, It knows exactly which action to take in any given state to maximize its rewards. For example, it has a smooth walking pattern without unnecessary tilts or falls

Real-World Example

Child learning to ride a bicycle

- At first, they try random things like pedaling hard, leaning too far, or braking abruptly.
- Over time, they learn which actions keep them balanced and moving smoothly.
- Eventually, they ride effortlessly without falling, having refined their "policy" through experience.

In this chapter, we explored the fundamental ways machines learn: supervised learning, unsupervised learning, and reinforcement learning. These approaches form the foundation of machine learning and are widely used in real-world applications. However, the learning process does not stop here—hybrid approaches and advanced paradigms such as semi-supervised learning, self-supervised learning, and transfer learning push the boundaries of what machines can achieve.

Choosing the right learning paradigm depends on the task type and data availability. For labeled data, supervised learning is effective, while unsupervised learning is ideal for identifying hidden patterns. Reinforcement learning excels in sequential decision-making tasks, and paradigms like self-supervised and few-shot learning provide solutions when labeled data is scarce, making them invaluable for specific challenges.

These diverse paradigms demonstrate the flexibility and adaptability of machine learning systems, enabling them to tackle a wide range of problems. Whether optimizing a search algorithm, creating personalized recommendations, or solving dynamic tasks, the right learning approach ensures machines perform efficiently and effectively.

CHAPTER FOUR

AI Models

An AI model is a computational framework or algorithm designed to process data, recognize patterns, and generate predictions or decisions based on given inputs. AI models have revolutionized modern technology by enabling machines to perform tasks such as creating content and forecasting outcomes from data. These models play a pivotal role in advancing industries like healthcare, entertainment, and finance, highlighting their versatility and transformative impact. Among the various types of AI models, two primary categories—generative and predictive—stand out for driving significant innovations across these domains.

Generative models create new, realistic data similar to the original dataset, while predictive models focus on forecasting outcomes or trends based on existing data. From generating realistic images with tools like DALL·E to predicting customer churn in businesses, both types play critical roles in solving diverse challenges across industries.

These models complement each other in many real-world scenarios, often working together to achieve complex goals. For example, generative models can simulate data for training predictive models, improving accuracy when real-world data is limited.

Generative AI Models

An AI - Illustration of Generative AI

Generative models are AI systems designed to create new data that closely resembles the patterns and structures of their training data. Unlike predictive models that analyze and forecast, generative models focus on producing content, such as images, text, or music based on learned data distributions. Their primary purpose is to enable machines to exhibit creativity and generate realistic outputs.

How Gen AI Relate to Deep Learning

Generative models leverage advanced deep learning architectures, such as Generative Adversarial Networks (GANs), Variational Autoencoders (VAEs), and Transformers, to achieve their goals. GANs use a generator-discriminator framework to produce high-quality outputs, while VAEs focus on generating data through probabilistic methods. Transformers, as seen in models like GPT, excel at generating coherent text and other sequential data, demonstrating the versatility of deep learning in generative tasks.

Applications

Generative models have revolutionized various industries with their applications. In art generation, they create digital artwork, realistic images, and even animations. Synthetic data generation provides large datasets for training other machine learning models, especially in fields like healthcare and finance. Text-to-image models like DALL·E have opened new possibilities for creative design by transforming textual descriptions into vivid visuals. In natural language processing (NLP), models like GPT are used for tasks such as content creation, chatbots, and storytelling, showcasing the adaptability of generative approaches.

Advantages

Generative models unlock creativity and innovation in tasks where realism and imagination are essential. They enable the creation of content that mimics human-like ingenuity, such as producing realistic virtual environments or designing new products. Their ability to fill gaps in data, generate unique outputs, and drive immersive experiences makes them invaluable in media creation, gaming, and virtual reality applications. Through these capabilities, generative models continue to redefine the boundaries of AI-driven creativity.

Few Generative AI Models Examples

Stable Diffusion

- Organization: Stability AI
- Type: Diffusion-based generative model.
- Purpose: Generates high-quality images from text prompts.
- Applications: Artistic content creation, photorealistic image generation, and design prototyping.

Runway ML

- Organization: Runway AI
- Type: Platform utilizing GANs and diffusion-based models.
- Purpose: Enables video and image editing with AI-assisted effects and creative transformations.
- Applications: Content editing, video effects, and generative media workflows.

DeepFake Models

- Developed by various open-source groups
- Type: GAN-based generative model.
- Purpose: Specializes in face and video manipulation, creating hyper-realistic outputs.
- Applications: Entertainment, synthetic video creation, and virtual avatars (with ethical concerns).

Tech stack for building Generative AI Models

To develop and deploy generative AI solutions, a robust technology stack is essential. Below is an overview of few key components widely used in building generative AI systems

- **Python:** Python continues to dominate as the preferred programming language for AI development, thanks to its rich ecosystem of libraries like NumPy, Pandas, and SciPy. Its simplicity and community support make it ideal for building and experimenting with generative AI models.
- **TensorFlow and PyTorch:** These deep learning frameworks remain the backbone of generative AI development. TensorFlow offers scalability and production-ready tools, while PyTorch excels in flexibility and ease of prototyping, making both indispensable for model training and deployment.
- **Hugging Face:** Hugging Face has become a go-to platform for generative AI, offering a vast repository of pre-trained models, including those for text generation, image synthesis, and audio creation. Its user-friendly interface and APIs significantly reduce development time.
- **CUDA and cuDNN:** NVIDIA's GPU-accelerated libraries, CUDA and cuDNN, are critical for speeding up training processes. These tools optimize the performance of complex generative models, particularly when handling large datasets and high-resolution outputs.
- **OpenAI API:** OpenAI's platform provides access to advanced generative models such as DALL·E and GPT. Developers can integrate these APIs into applications for generating images, text, and other creative outputs with minimal overhead.
- **Unity's ML-Agents Toolkit:** Unity has expanded its Machine Learning Agents Toolkit, enabling the integration of generative AI into 3D environments. This is particularly useful for game development, virtual simulations, and interactive storytelling.

Predictive Models

Predictive models are AI systems designed to analyze historical data, uncover patterns, and forecast future outcomes, aiding in informed decision-making. By analyzing input variables and their relationships to target outcomes, these models use statistical and mathematical techniques to estimate future events. Their purpose is to reduce uncertainty, identify trends, and enhance decision-making for businesses and individuals. The accuracy of predictions depends on the complexity of the data and the algorithms employed. Below key examples

- **Linear Regression:** Used for predicting numerical values, such as stock prices or sales trends.
  Example: Forecasting a company's revenue based on past performance.
- **Decision Trees and Random Forests:** Effective for classification and regression tasks.
  Example: Identifying customers likely to churn or determining loan approval likelihood.
- **Neural Networks for Prediction:** Ideal for handling complex and high-dimensional data. Example: Weather forecasting by analyzing historical weather patterns, or diagnosing diseases based on patient data.

Real-World Applications

Predictive models power numerous real-world use cases across industries. In finance, they are used for fraud detection by analyzing transaction patterns. Retail businesses rely on them for demand forecasting to manage inventory effectively. They enable personalized recommendations in e-commerce and streaming platforms, enhancing user experiences.

Few Predictive AI Models Examples

Linear Regression

- Open Source, **Type:** Statistical/machine learning model.
- **Purpose:** Predicts numerical outcomes based on relationships between variables.
- **Applications:** Stock price prediction, sales forecasting, and trend analysis.

Random Forest

- Open Source, **Type:** learning model using decision trees
- **Purpose:** Predicts outcomes by aggregating results from multiple decision trees
- **Applications:** Customer churn prediction, loan approval, and fraud detection

Neural Networks for Prediction

- **Organization:** Originated in academic research and was later popularized by frameworks like TensorFlow (Google) and PyTorch (Meta).
- **Type:** Deep learning model.
- **Purpose:** Predicts outcomes from complex, high-dimensional data by identifying non-linear patterns.
- **Applications:** Weather forecasting, healthcare diagnostics (e.g., disease prediction), and demand forecasting.

Tech Stack For Building Predictive AI Models

Predictive AI models continue to leverage advanced tools and frameworks to analyze data, identify patterns, and forecast outcomes. Below is a overview of the few key components.

- **Python:** Python remains the backbone of predictive AI due to its extensive libraries and community support. Key libraries like Scikit-learn for traditional machine learning, Pandas for data manipulation, NumPy for numerical computations, and Statsmodels for statistical modeling remain indispensable.
- **Deep Learning Frameworks (TensorFlow and PyTorch):** These frameworks extend beyond deep learning to predictive modeling. Time series forecasting, sequential prediction, and predictive healthcare diagnostics are now commonly implemented with deep architectures like LSTMs, GRUs, and transformers. PyTorch continues to lead for research-oriented workflows, while TensorFlow dominates enterprise deployments with its TensorFlow Extended (TFX) pipeline.
- **Tableau and Power BI:** These visualization tools are critical for presenting predictive insights to stakeholders. By connecting to predictive models, they enable interactive dashboards and real-time decision-making.
- **BigQuery and Snowflake:** Cloud-based data warehousing platforms like Google BigQuery and Snowflake enable scalable data processing and integration with predictive models. They are crucial for organizations dealing with large-scale data predictions.
- AutoML Tools (H2O.ai, DataRobot, Google Vertex AI)
- Cloud-Based Platforms (Azure ML, AWS SageMaker, GCP AI Platform)
- Big Data Tools (BigQuery, Snowflake, Databricks)
- And R, XGBoost, LightGBM, and CatBoost

Custom AI Models

A Custom AI model is an AI system tailored to meet the specific needs of a particular application, business, or problem domain. Unlike pre-built general-purpose models (e.g., GPT, DALL·E), custom AI models are designed, trained, and optimized on unique datasets relevant to a specific task or industry. They are often built to address challenges that generic models cannot effectively solve or to align closely with an organization's goals. Key Characteristics includes

- **Tailored Training Data:** Custom AI models are trained on proprietary or domain-specific data to ensure accuracy and relevance for the intended use
- **Specialized Objectives:** They are designed to perform a particular task, such as predicting customer behavior, detecting anomalies, or generating domain-specific content.
- **Optimized Architecture:** The architecture of the model can be fine-tuned (e.g., by modifying neural network layers or hyperparameters) to maximize performance for the specific application.

Building a Custom AI model

- Define the Problem, Collect Relevant Data, Choose or Develop Architecture, Train and Fine-Tune, Test and Evaluate.

Custom AI models are essential when off-the-shelf solutions cannot adequately meet the unique demands of a specific problem or business case.

More AI Models

Beyond Predictive and Generative AI models, there are other types of AI models designed to address specific tasks and challenges, a few of which are mentioned below. These models highlight the diversity of AI applications and their ability to cater to unique industry needs and technological advancements..

Conversational AI Models

- **Purpose:** Enable machines to understand and respond to human language interactively.
- **Focus:** Dialogue generation and natural language understanding.
- **Examples:** ChatGPT (OpenAI): Conversational LLM for chat-based interactions. Google Bard: AI for search-focused and conversational tasks.
- **Applications:** Customer service, virtual assistants, and interactive education.

Multimodal AI Models

- **Purpose:** Process and integrate multiple types of data (e.g., text, images, audio, video)
- **Focus:** Understanding and generating outputs across modalities.
- **Examples:** CLIP (OpenAI): Links text and images for tasks like visual recognition and text-based image generation. DALL·E: Generates images from text prompts by integrating textual and visual data.
- **Applications:** Content creation, accessibility tools, and education.

Embodied AI Models

- **Purpose:** Integrate AI into physical systems like robots or IoT devices.
- **Focus:** Perception, interaction, and control in physical environments.
- **Examples:** Tesla's Optimus Robot: Performs household tasks and interactions.
- **Applications:** Robotics, smart homes, and autonomous vehicles.

Simulation AI Models

- **Purpose:** Simulate complex systems or environments to study behaviors and interactions.
- **Focus:** Virtual experimentation without real-world risks.
- **Examples:** Weather simulation models.Financial market simulators.
- **Applications:** Climate change studies, financial risk modeling, and urban planning

CHAPTER FIVE

LARGE LANGUAGE MODELS - LLM

Large Language Models (LLMs) are AI systems designed to process and generate human-like language by analyzing vast amounts of text. Built on transformer-based architectures, they excel in understanding grammar, semantics, and context, enabling tasks like answering questions, generating content, and facilitating natural conversations. LLMs have become pivotal in reshaping industries and human-AI interactions.

OpenAI's GPT series has driven the evolution of LLMs, with each iteration, from GPT-2 to GPT-4, expanding their capabilities. GPT-4, launched in 2023, introduced multimodal functionality and advanced reasoning, making ChatGPT and similar tools indispensable. These innovations have positioned LLMs as transformative technologies across business, education, and healthcare.

Unlike traditional rule-based AI, LLMs utilize vast datasets and deep learning to adapt across diverse tasks, their ability to generate accurate, contextually relevant outputs has revolutionized applications such as customer support, content creation, and advanced research, showcasing their broad and lasting impact.

ChatGPT

OpenAI developed ChatGPT as part of its efforts to advance natural language processing and make AI more accessible to the public. it was officially launched by OpenAI on November 30, 2022. ChatGPT quickly found applications across diverse fields, from content creation and customer support to coding assistance and educational tutoring. This versatility showcased the potential of conversational AI to transform multiple industries.

GPT stands for Generative Pre-trained Transformer. It is a type of AI model developed by OpenAI that generates human-like text based on input prompts. **"Generative"** refers to its ability to produce text, **"Pre-trained"** means it's trained on vast datasets before being fine-tuned for specific tasks, and **"Transformer"** refers to the neural network architecture it uses, which excels at understanding and generating language by processing context within text.

How it works

ChatGPT is powered by a transformer-based architecture, leveraging advancements in natural language processing. Its self-attention mechanisms enable the model to understand relationships between words in context, even when they are far apart in a sentence. By analyzing large datasets and continuously fine-tuning billions of parameters, it generates coherent, context-aware responses that mimic human conversation.

The training process includes massive datasets from diverse sources like books, articles, and websites, reflecting up-to-date language use. With powerful computational infrastructure, the model adjusts neural connections to enhance its predictive accuracy and adaptability. This allows ChatGPT to provide reliable and sophisticated human-like conversational outputs

ChatGPT: Versions, Models, and Capabilities

GPT-3 and GPT-3.5

- **Key Features:** GPT-3 introduced robust text generation, enabling tasks like summarization, translation, and creative writing. GPT-3.5 enhanced conversational coherence and reduced inconsistencies in responses.
- **Capabilities:** General knowledge queries. Creative content generation (poems, stories, and articles). Assisting with basic coding tasks and debugging.

GPT-4

- **Key Features:** Enhanced reasoning and contextual understanding. Introduced multimodal capabilities, processing both text and images in Pro versions.
- **Capabilities:** Solving technical problems in fields like programming, mathematics, and science. Generating detailed professional documents and reports. Assisting in creative brainstorming for businesses.

GPT-4o

- **Key Features:** Faster and more cost-efficient compared to GPT-4. Supports text, image, and audio processing, making it highly versatile.

- **Capabilities:** State-of-the-art performance in voice, multilingual, and vision benchmarks. Voice recognition and multilingual support. Enhanced vision-based tasks and conversational workflows. Ideal for both professional and personal use.

GPT-4o mini

- **Key Features:** A smaller, cost-effective version of GPT-4o optimized for lightweight applications.
- **Capabilities:** Designed for enterprises and startups seeking scalable AI solutions. Ideal for resource-constrained environments requiring automation and efficiency.

o1-Preview

- **Key Features:** Developed for advanced problem-solving with improved reasoning and accuracy. Excels in handling complex mathematical and scientific queries.
- **Capabilities:** Competitive programming. High-level reasoning tasks in technical and scientific domains. Performs well in fields requiring advanced analytical capabilities.

Conclusion

From GPT-3's revolutionary text generation to o1-Preview's advanced reasoning and problem-solving, ChatGPT continues to redefine the boundaries of conversational AI. Each iteration enhances its usability, versatility, and efficiency, empowering professionals, businesses.

Challenges and Limitations : Issues with LLM's

- **Bias and Ethical Concerns:** LLMs arise from the vast datasets used during training, which often contain biases present in real-world language. Since these models learn patterns from this data, they can inadvertently reproduce or amplify stereotypes and prejudiced views.
- **Misinformation:** LLMs sometimes generate responses that sound believable but are factually incorrect, a phenomenon known as "hallucination." This can lead to the spread of misinformation, especially if users rely on the model for accurate answers.
- **Data Privacy:** LLMs rely heavily on large datasets for training, which raises concerns about data privacy and security. Ensuring privacy involves strict data handling practices and exploring techniques like differential privacy to protect user information in AI systems.
- **Resource Intensity:** Training and operating large language models demand significant computational power and resources, leading to high energy consumption. This resource intensity contributes to environmental concerns due to the carbon footprint of data centers. As AI technology advances, there is a growing focus on optimizing models to reduce their energy requirements and improve efficiency.
- **Difficulty with Niche Knowledge:** While LLMs perform well on general knowledge, they may struggle with niche or specialized domains due to limited data exposure in these areas. This can lead to less accurate or incomplete responses when addressing specialized topics.

These challenges highlight the limitations and concerns that come with using large language models.

Tech Stack for Building Large Language Models (LLMs)

To develop and deploy Large Language Models (LLMs), a robust technology stack is essential. Below is an overview of key components widely used in building LLM systems:

- **Python:** Python remains the cornerstone for developing LLMs, thanks to its extensive ecosystem of libraries like NumPy, Pandas, and Scikit-learn. Its simplicity and widespread adoption make it a preferred choice for building and fine-tuning LLMs.
- **TensorFlow and PyTorch:** These frameworks dominate LLM development, providing powerful tools for training deep neural networks. TensorFlow excels in scalability and deployment, while PyTorch offers flexibility and ease of experimentation, making both integral to modern LLM projects.
- **Transformers Library:** Hugging Face's Transformers library is indispensable for LLMs, offering pre-built architectures like BERT, GPT, and T5. This library simplifies the process of implementing, fine-tuning, and deploying transformer-based models.
- **Distributed Training Frameworks:** Tools like Horovod and DeepSpeed are essential for training LLMs across multiple GPUs and nodes. These frameworks optimize resource utilization, reduce training time, and enable the scaling of massive models.
- **Tokenization Tools:** SentencePiece and Byte-Pair Encoding (BPE) are widely used for tokenizing text, converting raw input into manageable sequences. These tools ensure efficient data preprocessing for LLMs.
- And Cloud Platforms, Dataset Management Tools, CUDA and cuDNN etc.

These technology stack represents the backbone of LLM development. enabling researchers and developers to build state-of-the-art LLMs.

Few Large Language Models (LLMs) in 2024

GPT-4 (OpenAI)

- GPT-4, including its multimodal variant GPT-4 Vision, continues to lead the industry with its advanced reasoning, coding, and text-generation abilities. It supports both text and image inputs, making it a versatile model for complex applications.
- **Applications:** Content creation, coding assistance, customer service, and advanced data analysis.

Claude 3 (Anthropic)

- Claude is known for its safety-oriented design, focusing on ethical AI interactions and reliability. It emphasizes alignment with human values and aims to minimize harmful outputs
- **Applications:** Conversational AI, document summarization, and research assistance.

Gemini 1 (Google DeepMind)

- Gemini integrates multimodal capabilities (text, image, and audio) with Google's expertise in search and reinforcement learning. It's designed for contextual understanding and enhanced decision-making.
- **Applications:** Multimodal search, customer service, and interactive virtual assistants.

Real-World Applications of Large Language Models

Below are a few real-world applications of Large Language Models (LLMs), showcasing their versatility and transformative impact across industries.

- **Content Creation:** Writers leverage LLMs for drafting blogs, articles, and social media posts. Marketing teams use them for generating personalized advertisements, slogans, and engaging content that resonates with specific audiences.
- **Creative Arts:** In film, gaming, and design, LLMs assist in scriptwriting, character development, and creating immersive narratives. They contribute to crafting engaging storylines and dialogues.
- **Coding Assistance:** Developers rely on LLM-powered tools like GitHub Copilot for writing, debugging, and refactoring code. These models accelerate software development, reduce errors, and enhance productivity.
- **Healthcare:** These models summarize medical records, draft clinical notes, and assist in diagnosing symptoms. LLMs like GPT-4 enable doctors to quickly retrieve relevant research and simplify medical jargon for patients.
- **Legal and Compliance:** LLMs analyze legal documents, contracts, and compliance policies to identify risks or inconsistencies. They help draft agreements and provide quick references to laws and precedents.
- **Customer Support:** LLMs power AI chatbots that handle customer queries with speed and precision, providing 24/7 support. They assist in resolving issues, guiding users through processes, and offering product recommendations across industries like e-commerce, banking, and telecom.

The adaptability of LLMs across sectors demonstrates their pivotal role in revolutionizing tasks and unlocking new possibilities.

Enhancing LLMs with Retrieval-Augmented Generation (RAG)

Retrieval-Augmented Generation (RAG) is a powerful framework designed to enhance Large Language Models (LLMs) by combining their generative capabilities with real-time data retrieval. While traditional LLMs generate responses based on static, pre-trained knowledge, RAG introduces a retrieval step that fetches relevant, up-to-date information from external databases, search engines, or knowledge repositories during inference. This dynamic approach enables LLMs to generate more accurate and contextually relevant outputs.

RAG operates by integrating two key components

- **Retrieval Systems:** Tools like Elasticsearch, FAISS, or vector databases fetch relevant information from structured or unstructured knowledge sources, including documents, APIs, or wikis.
- **Generative Models:** Pre-trained LLMs, such as GPT-4 or BERT, use the retrieved data as context to produce coherent and precise responses, ensuring alignment with current knowledge..

The benefits of RAG include dynamic knowledge integration, reduced hallucination, enhanced domain adaptability, and improved relevance.

Enhancing LLMs with RAG represents a significant advancement in AI capabilities, bridging the gap between generative models and the need for real-time, accurate information. By combining retrieval systems with LLMs, RAG empowers businesses and researchers to solve domain-specific challenges, ensuring that AI outputs are both relevant and reliable.

Fine-Tuning LLMs for Specific Industries

Large Language Models (LLMs) are designed as general-purpose tools capable of understanding and generating human-like text across a wide range of domains. However, industries often have unique requirements that demand customization of these models for optimal performance. Fine-tuning LLMs involves adapting a pre-trained model to specific tasks or sectors by retraining it on domain-specific data, ensuring the output aligns with industry-specific needs.

AI Representation of Professionals Teaching a Computer

Why Fine-Tuning Matters

General-purpose LLMs excel at understanding and generating human-like text, but industries often require more nuanced and contextual responses. For instance, the healthcare industry demands expertise in medical terminology, while the legal sector relies on precise interpretation of laws and contracts. Fine-tuning ensures the LLM understands and applies this domain-specific knowledge effectively.

Steps in Fine-Tuning LLMs

- **Data Collection:** Gather high-quality, domain-specific datasets relevant to the industry. For example, financial reports for banking or clinical notes for healthcare.
- **Training Adjustments:** Adapt the pre-trained model using fine-tuning frameworks like Hugging Face Transformers or OpenAI's API. These tools help retain general language understanding while optimizing for industry-specific nuances.
- **Evaluation and Feedback:** Test the fine-tuned model on real-world tasks to evaluate its performance, followed by iterative refinements based on feedback.

Industry Applications

- Healthcare: Fine-tuned LLMs can assist in summarizing patient records, generating medical reports, and supporting diagnostic insights.
- Legal: Industry-specific models can draft contracts, analyze case law, and ensure compliance with regulations.

- Finance: Customized LLMs can generate market analysis, forecast trends, and streamline customer interactions with personalized financial advice.
- Education: Fine-tuning allows LLMs to create industry-specific learning content, tailor lesson plans, and automate student evaluations.

Technology and Tools

The fine-tuning process leverages frameworks like TensorFlow, PyTorch, and Hugging Face. Advanced techniques such as parameter-efficient fine-tuning (e.g., LoRA) and reinforcement learning ensure efficient adaptation with minimal computational overhead, making the process scalable for businesses of all sizes.

Fine-tuning LLMs for specific industries unlocks their full potential, turning generalized capabilities into precise, targeted solutions. By bridging the gap between versatility and specificity, this approach empowers businesses to address their unique challenges and achieve significant advancements across sectors.

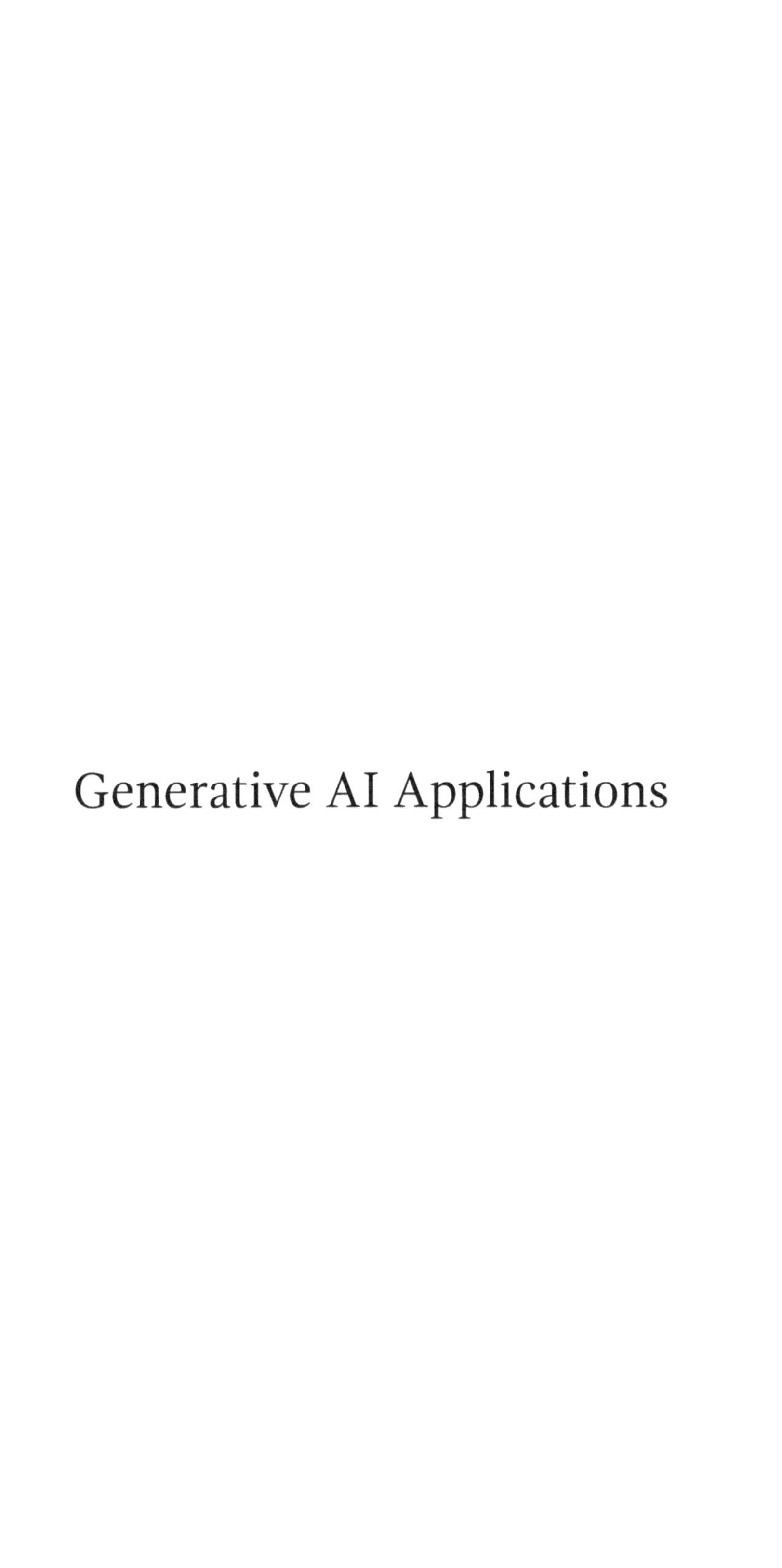

Generative AI Applications

CHAPTER SIX

TEXT TO IMAGE

Generative AI - Text-to-Image is a cutting-edge technology that turns textual descriptions into visually accurate and creative images. It combines natural language processing with advanced computer vision, enabling seamless translation of words into visuals.

Example - AI Generated Text to Image

This innovation is revolutionizing industries like design and entertainment by allowing rapid visualization of ideas. From photorealistic renders to artistic concepts.

Popular Text-to-Image Models

DALLE-2 (OpenAI): Developed by OpenAI, DALLE-2 continues to lead in generating high-quality, contextually accurate images from textual descriptions. It incorporates advanced features like inpainting and image compositionality, enabling users to modify and customize visuals. Applications span advertising, design, and concept visualization, cementing its role in creative industries and education.

Stable Diffusion (Stability AI): As an open-source powerhouse, Stable Diffusion remains a preferred choice for developers and creators in 2024. Its flexibility and customization options allow users to generate photorealistic and stylized images for diverse use cases, including game development, content creation, and virtual environments. Its thriving community continues to drive innovation and accessibility.

MidJourney: MidJourney has solidified its position as a tool for generating artistic and imaginative visuals. Its unique ability to create surreal and stylized content makes it ideal for branding, storytelling, and creative expression. The platform's focus on community engagement fosters collaboration and inspires users to experiment with artistic designs.

Imagen (Google): Google's Imagen stands out for its capability to generate photorealistic images with fine-grained control. By focusing on details and contextual alignment, Imagen is particularly useful for industries like e-commerce, product design, and marketing. Its precision and fidelity ensure outputs meet high-quality standards, aligning with specific user needs.

These are a few models that represent the cutting edge of generative AI in 2024.

Sytles of AI Generated Images

Gen AI text-to-image tools can create images in various styles

Styles : HD, Kodak, Semi-realistic, Animated, Artistic and More

Example of AI Generated Realistic Image

Process of Building Text-to-Image Models

- **Choose the Model Architecture** : Diffusion Models for high-quality and diverse image generation. GANs (Generative Adversarial Networks) for stylized or artistic outputs. Transformers for context-aware and flexible generation.
- **Prepare the Training Dataset** : Gather and preprocess a large dataset of image-text pairs from sources like. Public datasets such as COCO, Flickr30k, or LAION-5B. Domain-specific datasets for specialized use cases (e.g., annotated medical images).
- **Tokenize the Text Input** : Break the input text into smaller parts (tokens) using NLP techniques. Apply models like BERT, GPT, or CLIP to convert these tokens into numerical representations that capture their meaning.
- **Encode Image Features** : Use pre-trained vision models like ResNet or Vision Transformers (ViT) to extract image features and represent them numerically. This step aligns visual features with the text.
- **Map to Latent Space** : Train the model to align text and image features in a shared latent space. This ensures the model can generate images that accurately represent the input descriptions.
- **Implement Attention Mechanisms** : Incorporate attention layers (as in transformers) to focus on critical elements in the text. For example, the phrase "vibrant orange skies" is emphasized during image generation.
- **Train the Model** : Train the model using supervised learning and generative techniques.
- Further refine the model through fine-tuning, integrate quality evaluation mechanisms, optimize and deploy the system, and conduct thorough testing with iterative improvements.

Technology Stack for Building Text-to-Image Models

General tech stack used for building text-to-image models

- **Python:** Python is the cornerstone of text-to-image model development, valued for its simplicity and the robust ecosystem of libraries it offers. Frameworks like TensorFlow and PyTorch are indispensable for implementing cutting-edge architectures such as diffusion models and GANs. Additionally, Hugging Face Transformers play a pivotal role in integrating natural language processing (NLP) with computer vision seamlessly.
- **NLP Frameworks:** Text encoders like CLIP, GPT, and T5 are at the heart of converting textual prompts into numerical representations. These embeddings align with visual features, enabling precise mapping between text descriptions and the corresponding generated images.
- **Vision Transformers (ViT):** Vision Transformers and 3D Convolutional Neural Networks (3D CNNs) are critical for extracting and analyzing visual features. These technologies allow models to accurately interpret and replicate complex visual details, bridging the gap between text input and visual output.
- **Distributed Training:** Tools such as Horovod and DeepSpeed are integral for distributed training, enabling the efficient use of multiple GPUs. This approach optimizes resource utilization, reduces training times, and ensures scalability, which is particularly vital for training large-scale models like Stable Diffusion.
- **NVIDIA GPUs and CUDA:** The computational demands of text-to-image models require the high efficiency provided by NVIDIA GPUs, powered by CUDA. These tools are essential for managing the vast datasets and intricate algorithms that drive generative models, ensuring rapid and reliable training processes.

How Text-to-Image Models Works

- **Input the Text :** Provide a description (e.g., "a cat sitting on a red chair").
- **Text Processing :** The model breaks the text into smaller parts (tokens) and converts them into numerical data.
- **Text Encoding :** The tokenized text is encoded into a numerical representation (latent vector) that captures its meaning and context.
- **Attention Mechanism :** Use attention layers to focus on key parts of the input, ensuring that important details like "cat sitting" and "red chair" are emphasized in the encoding.
- **Shared Latent Space :** The encoded text is mapped into a shared latent space, where it aligns with visual concepts and features.
- **Pre-Trained Knowledge Integration:** Leverage knowledge from pre-trained models (e.g., DALL-E, Stable Diffusion) to generate an initial draft of the image, informed by millions of prior examples.
- **Decoding into an Image :** Decode the latent representation into an image using neural networks, such as GANs or diffusion models.
- **Refinement and Post-Processing :** The generated image is fine-tuned and adjusted to ensure it matches the text prompt accurately and visually.
- **Quality Evaluation :** Evaluate the image using a feedback mechanism or scoring system to check coherence, relevance, and quality compared to the input text.
- **Output the Image :** The final image is produced and delivered to the user, reflecting the details and style described in the prompt.

This workflow reflects the state-of-the-art advancements in text-to-image models as of 2024, incorporating their ability to generate high-quality, contextually aligned visuals with precision

Real-World Implementations of Text-to-Image Models

Text-to-image models have moved beyond research labs to real-world applications, transforming industries with their ability to generate high-quality visuals from textual descriptions.

- **Marketing and Advertising** : Brands and Small and Medium Businesses, leverage text-to-image models to create visually compelling advertisements, promotional materials and AI influencers without the need for expensive photoshoots, reducing costs and accelerating campaign timelines.
- **E-Commerce** : These models enable dynamic product visualization. Retailers can generate custom images of products in various settings. For example, a furniture store might generate visuals of a sofa in different room styles and lighting conditions, helping customers envision how the product will look in their own homes.
- **Education** : Text-to-image models enhance learning by creating illustrative content for textbooks and online courses. For instance, educators can use prompts like "the lifecycle of a butterfly" to generate step-by-step visuals that improve comprehension and engagement in classrooms.
- **Film & Entertainment** : These models are used for character and dreature design, set and environment design, poster and promotional material design.
- **Social Media** : Social media platforms and content creators use these models to generate engaging visuals for posts and videos.
- **Journalism and Media** : Creating illustrative content for news articles, stories, or editorials to make them visually appealing.
- **Creating Synthetic Data** : Text-to-Image models are increasingly used to generate synthetic data for training other AI systems, particularly in scenarios where real-world data is scarce, expensive, or sensitive.

Example : AI Generated Image for Jeans Brand

Text-to-image AI models symbolize the fusion of creativity and technology, unlocking a new realm where words seamlessly transform into visuals. These advancements empower industries to innovate, enabling not just faster workflows but entirely new ways to visualize ideas and communicate concepts.

As the technology evolves, it holds the promise to democratize artistic expression, bridge gaps between imagination and execution, and redefine standards of storytelling and design. These are not just tools—they are catalysts shaping the future of visual creativity.

CHAPTER SEVEN

TEXT TO VIDEO

Generative AI - Text-to-Video represents the next frontier in content creation, transforming textual descriptions into dynamic, high-quality video clips. By blending natural language processing with advanced video synthesis.

AI Text to Video

This innovation is revolutionizing fields like entertainment, education, and marketing by offering rapid visualization of ideas. From cinematic scenes to instructional videos, the applications are expansive and impactful.

Popular Text-to-Video Models

- **Sora (OpenAI):** is capable of generating high-quality videos from simple text prompts, pushing the boundaries of text-to-video technology. enabling creators to produce visually realistic content, opening new possibilities for storytelling and visual media
- **Make-A-Video (Meta):** Developed by Meta, this model focuses on producing creative and high-quality videos from textual inputs. It finds use in advertising, creative content production, and personalized video campaigns.
- **Runway Gen-3 Alpha Turbo:** is an advanced AI model designed for generating high-quality, realistic videos with improved speed and precision. It empowers creators to produce dynamic and lifelike visuals.
- **Imagen Video (Google):** Imagen Video builds upon Google's Imagen framework, producing highly realistic and contextually accurate video clips. It caters to applications in education, e-commerce, and immersive marketing.

Styles of AI-Generated Videos

AI-generated videos span a variety of styles, from realistic and cinematic to animated and artistic, offering versatile applications in storytelling, branding, education, and entertainment.

- Realistic: Captures life-like details with high fidelity.
- Cinematic: Creates professional, film-quality sequences.
- Animated: Ideal for explainer videos and storytelling.
- Artistic: Focuses on surreal and creative video outputs.
- Abstract: Delivers experimental or conceptual visuals.

Process of Building Text-to-Video Models

General framework for building text-to-video models

- **Choose the Model Architecture:** Advanced architectures such as diffusion models are used for generating photorealistic outputs, while GANs (Generative Adversarial Networks) are ideal for producing stylized and creative videos.
- **Prepare the Training Dataset:** Large video-text datasets are gathered and preprocessed. These datasets are often supplemented with domain-specific content to meet specialized requirements.
- **Tokenize the Text Input:** Input text is processed into tokens using Natural Language Processing (NLP) frameworks such as GPT or T5, breaking the text into smaller components for efficient analysis and understanding.
- **Encode Video Frames:** Visual features are extracted from video frames using specialized architectures like 3D CNNs (e.g., I3D, C3D) or TimeSformer models, which are designed to handle temporal video data effectively.
- **Map to Latent Space:** Text and video data are aligned in a shared latent space, creating a unified representation that ensures coherence between the input text and the generated video.
- **Implement Temporal Attention:** Attention mechanisms are applied to maintain smooth transitions between video frames, ensuring the temporal flow and continuity of the generated video.
- **Train the Model:** Training is conducted using supervised or self-supervised learning techniques. Additional fine-tuning is performed with targeted datasets to address specific industry use cases, such as marketing or education.
- **Optimize and Deploy:** enhance efficiency, scalability, reliability.

Technology Stack for Building Text-to-Video Models

General tech stack used for building text-to-video models.

- **Python:** Python remains the foundation for text-to-video model development, offering robust libraries and frameworks. TensorFlow and PyTorch support the creation of advanced architectures like temporal GANs and diffusion models, while Hugging Face Transformers bridge natural language processing (NLP) with video generation.
- **NLP Frameworks:** Text encoders such as CLIP, GPT, and T5 convert textual descriptions into numerical embeddings. These embeddings align text input with video outputs, ensuring semantic consistency and preserving the meaning of the original prompt
- **Temporal Video Models:** Models like TimeSformer and 3D Convolutional Neural Networks (3D CNNs) are essential for understanding motion dynamics and generating sequential frames. These architectures maintain smooth transitions between frames and capture intricate temporal relationships.
- **Distributed Training:** Tools like DeepSpeed and Horovod optimize distributed training across multiple GPUs, enabling efficient resource utilization. This scalability is crucial for training large video models with extensive datasets.
- **NVIDIA GPUs and CUDA:** The computational power of NVIDIA GPUs, driven by CUDA, is indispensable for handling the massive datasets and complex calculations involved in video generation. These tools ensure fast and efficient processing for real-time frame synthesis and training.
- **Pre-trained Models:** Frameworks like Phenaki, Runway Gen-2, Imagen Video, and Make-A-Video provide a strong starting point for developers. These models can be fine-tuned for industry-specific video generation, significantly reducing development time and enhancing performance

How Text-to-Video Models Work

- **Input the Text:** Begin with a descriptive prompt, such as "a group of traditional Arab men playing music in a desert tent," which provides the model with clear guidance on the scene to generate.
- **Text Processing:** The text prompt is tokenized and encoded into numerical representations using NLP models like GPT or T5. Key details like "Arab men," "playing music," and "desert tent" are captured to inform the visual and thematic aspects of the video.
- **Shared Latent Space:** The encoded text is mapped into a shared latent space where the semantic elements (e.g., cultural attire, musical instruments, and the desert setting) align with corresponding video features.
- **Video Frame Generation:** Advanced models like GANs or diffusion models generate individual frames. The initial frames might depict a desert tent at sunset, transitioning to the men playing traditional instruments like ouds or darbukas under warm lantern light.
- **Temporal Coherence:** Temporal attention mechanisms ensure consistency across frames, such as the rhythmic movements of the musicians and the flickering of lanterns, maintaining smooth playback throughout the sequence.
- **Post-Processing:** The video is refined to enhance visual details, such as the texture of the desert sand, intricate patterns on traditional clothing, and the glow of lanterns illuminating the scene.
- **Output the Video:** The final output is a high-quality, visually detailed video of "a group of traditional Arab men playing music in a desert tent," complete with cultural authenticity and aesthetic appeal, suitable for storytelling or cultural representation.

Real-World Implementations of Text-to-Video Models

- **Marketing and Advertising:** Enables the creation of dynamic video advertisements and personalized promotional content.
- **Education:** Facilitates the production of engaging instructional videos, making complex topics visually accessible.
- **Entertainment:** Supports animation, movie pre-visualization, and short film production from textual storylines.
- **Social Media:** Allows creators to generate vibrant, short-form video content.
- **Healthcare:** Generates instructional medical videos for training and patient education.
- **Synthetic Data Creation:** Produces video datasets for training AI systems in areas like autonomous driving and robotics.

As this technology continues to advance, it promises to unlock new dimensions of storytelling, allowing individuals and businesses to convey ideas with unprecedented clarity and creativity.

IMAGE TO VIDEO

An innovative technology that transforms static images into dynamic, visually compelling videos. By integrating advanced machine learning techniques with computer vision, it enables the seamless creation of animated sequences from still visuals.

Example : Image to Video

This innovation is revolutionizing fields like marketing, education, and entertainment by bringing static imagery to life. From creating product showcases to generating dynamic social media content, it allows for highly engaging storytelling.

Popular Image-to-Video Models

- Runway Gen-2 (RunwayML): Known for its advanced editing capabilities and cinematic outputs, this model excels in transforming single images into videos with smooth transitions and detailed animations
- DeepMind's FrameGen: This model leverages advanced temporal attention mechanisms to create realistic motion from a sequence of images.
- Pika Labs: Specializes in turning static product images into short, creative video advertisements tailored for e-commerce and digital platforms.
- Imagen Video (Google): Builds on Google's Imagen framework to generate photorealistic, contextually accurate video clips for diverse applications like education and marketing.
- Phenaki (Google): Phenaki excels in generating long-duration videos from a combination of image and text prompts. Its ability to maintain contextual coherence over extended sequences makes it a powerful tool for storytelling, educational videos, and documentaries
- D-ID Creative Reality Studio: Specializing in face animation technology, this platform transforms static portraits into videos with dynamic facial movements, often used for interactive marketing campaigns and character-based storytelling.

Styles of AI-Generated Videos

- Realistic: Captures life-like details with high fidelity.
- Cinematic: Produces professional, film-quality sequences.
- Animated: Ideal for creating explainer or educational videos.
- Artistic: Focuses on surreal, experimental, or creative outputs.

Process of Building Image-to-Video Models

- **Choose the Model Architecture:** Select advanced architectures such as GANs (Generative Adversarial Networks) or diffusion models to create high-quality video outputs from static images. These architectures are known for their ability to generate visually appealing and coherent animations.
- **Prepare the Training Dataset:** Curate large-scale datasets like the BAIR Robot Pushing dataset or VideoGAN datasets. These datasets provide image-video pairs essential for teaching the model to understand motion dynamics and temporal consistency.
- **Extract Image Features:** Leverage Vision Transformers (ViT) or 3D Convolutional Neural Networks (3D CNNs) to extract intricate details and features from static images. This step ensures the model captures all visual aspects required for realistic video generation.
- **Temporal Mapping:** Align the extracted features over a timeline to simulate smooth transitions between frames. Temporal mapping is critical to achieving realistic and fluid motion in the generated video.
- **Implement Temporal Attention:** Integrate temporal attention mechanisms to maintain spatial and temporal coherence across video frames. This step ensures that objects, textures, and movements remain consistent and natural throughout the video.
- **Train the Model:** Use supervised or unsupervised learning techniques to train the model. Fine-tuning on specific tasks or datasets can further improve the performance for niche applications, such as marketing videos or artistic animations.
- **Post-Processing:** Apply refinement techniques like super-resolution to enhance video quality. This step ensures that the output videos meet the desired resolution and visual standards.

Technology Stack for Building Image-to-Video Models

General tech stack used for building Image-to-video models

- **Python:** Python remains the backbone of image-to-video model development, offering simplicity and extensive support through libraries like TensorFlow and PyTorch. These libraries streamline the implementation of advanced machine learning algorithms for generating high-quality video outputs.
- **Vision Transformers (ViT):** ViT plays a crucial role in extracting static image features and aligning them to create coherent video sequences. By leveraging their ability to capture detailed visual patterns, ViTs bridge the gap between static images and dynamic video frames.
- **Temporal Networks:** Advanced frameworks like TimeSformer ensure smooth transitions across frames, maintaining temporal coherence and delivering videos with realistic and seamless motion. These networks align temporal data to ensure videos are both visually appealing and natural.
- **Distributed Training Platforms:** Platforms like Horovod and DeepSpeed enable scalable training across multiple GPUs, optimizing resource utilization and significantly reducing training time. These tools are essential for training large-scale models efficiently.
- **NVIDIA GPUs and CUDA:** NVIDIA GPUs, powered by CUDA, provide the computational efficiency required for training resource-intensive image-to-video models. Their parallel processing capabilities are vital for handling large datasets and complex neural network operations.
- **Pre-trained Models:** Foundational models like FrameGen and Imagen Video provide a starting point for developers. By fine-tuning these pre-trained architectures, developers can achieve faster deployment and better results without building models entirely from scratch.

How Image-to-Video Models Work

Image-to-video models convert static images into dynamic video sequences by analyzing visual elements and simulating realistic motion.

- **Input the Image:** Start with a single image or a sequence of images as input, such as a still photo of a man riding a camel in the desert.
- **Feature Extraction:** The model identifies key visual elements, including the camel, rider, flowing scarf, and the desert background, to capture the essence of the scene.
- **Temporal Mapping:** Visual features like the movement of the scarf and the camel's gait are mapped into a timeline, simulating natural motion.
- **Frame Generation:** Intermediate frames are generated to depict smooth transitions, such as the camel walking and the scarf fluttering in the wind.
- **Motion Refinement:** Adjustments are made to ensure realistic and coherent movements across frames, creating a lifelike representation of the desert scene.
- **Post-Processing:** Super-resolution and other refinement techniques are applied to enhance the quality of the video, ensuring high detail and clarity.
- **Output the Video:** The final output is a dynamic video showing the man riding the camel through the desert, with smooth, engaging motion and an immersive experience.

This workflow showcases the transformation of a static image into an animated sequence, emphasizing the potential of image-to-video technology in 2024 for storytelling, marketing, and creative applications.

Real-World Implementations of Image-to-Video Models

- **Marketing and Advertising:** Converts static product images into dynamic promotional videos, enhancing engagement and driving brand visibility.
- **Education:** Creates visually appealing animated videos from static diagrams or illustrations, simplifying the learning process for students.
- **Entertainment:** Brings still images to life for movie pre-visualization, short film sequences, and dynamic storytelling.
- **Social Media:** Transforms photos into engaging video content for reels, stories, and posts, capturing audience attention.
- **E-Commerce:** Animates product images to showcase features, creating immersive shopping experiences for customers.
- **Synthetic Data Creation:** Produces video datasets for AI training in robotics, self-driving cars, and other domains requiring motion understanding.

Image-to-Video AI models bridge the gap between static visuals and dynamic storytelling, enabling the creation of lifelike animations and immersive experiences. These models are revolutionizing content creation workflows, empowering industries with cost-effective and innovative video solutions.

As advancements in this technology continue, they unlock new possibilities for creative expression, allowing individuals and organizations to breathe life into still imagery with unprecedented clarity and impact.

TEXT TO MUSIC

Generative AI - AI Music is a revolutionary technology that creates original compositions and sounds based on input parameters. By analyzing patterns in existing music, it generates melodies, harmonies, and rhythms, transforming the way music is composed, produced, and experienced.

An AI-Generated Illustration of AI Music

This innovation is reshaping industries like entertainment, gaming, and advertising by offering customizable music solutions. From creating background scores to personalized soundtracks.

Popular AI Music Models

- **AIVA (Artificial Intelligence Virtual Artist):** AIVA remains a leading AI tool for creating emotional and dynamic soundtracks for films, video games, commercials, and personal projects. It tailors music to specific moods, themes, and genres, making it a favorite among content creators and game developers for its expressiveness and adaptability.
- **Magenta's MusicVAE:** MusicVAE is a deep learning model that focuses on generating and transforming melodies. It excels at creating variations of musical sequences, offering creative tools for melody generation, interpolation, and music-based experimentation.
- **MuseNet:** MuseNet is a deep learning model capable of generating 4-minute compositions with up to 10 instruments across various styles, including classical, pop, and jazz. It leverages its understanding of complex harmonies and compositions to create intricate and diverse musical outputs.(Note : This is retired but worth mentioning)
- **Google's Magenta:** is an open-source project using machine learning to enhance creativity in music and art, generating new melodies and lyrics by blending patterns from existing works.

Styles of AI-Generated Music

- **Classical:** Symphonies and orchestral arrangements.
- **Electronic:** Synth-based beats and ambient sounds.
- **Pop:** Catchy melodies and rhythmic patterns.
- **Jazz:** Improvised harmonies and syncopated rhythms.
- **Experimental:** Avant-garde and abstract soundscapes.

Process of Building AI Music Models

- **Select the Model Architecture:** Choose architectures such as Recurrent Neural Networks (RNNs), Generative Adversarial Networks (GANs), or Transformer-based models, which are well-suited for capturing temporal patterns and complexities in music.
- **Prepare the Training Dataset:** Collect and preprocess extensive datasets of MIDI files or audio samples from diverse genres to provide the model with a rich variety of musical patterns.
- **Data Augmentation:** Enhance the training dataset by applying techniques like pitch shifting, tempo changes, or introducing noise to improve the model's robustness and generalization.
- **Tokenize Musical Inputs:** Convert musical components like notes, rhythms, and dynamics into numerical representations (tokens) that can be processed by machine learning models.
- **Train the Model:** Use supervised learning to guide the model with labeled datasets or unsupervised learning to let the model discover patterns independently, enabling coherent music generation.
- **Incorporate Style Transfer:** Implement techniques that allow the model to emulate specific musical genres, instruments, or the styles of particular artists.
- **Enable Customization:** Design the model to allow users to customize inputs like genre, tempo, mood, or instruments, offering greater creative control.
- **Post-Process Outputs:** Refine the generated music with audio engineering techniques such as mixing and mastering to enhance quality and ensure a polished final output.
- **Optimize for Deployment:** Adapt the model for real-time music generation by ensuring low latency and scalability across platforms, making it suitable for applications like live performances, content creation, or consumer apps.

Technology Stack for Building Text to Music Models

General tech stack used for building Text to Muisc models.

- **Python**: Python: The foundational programming language for AI music development, equipped with powerful libraries like LibROSA for audio analysis and TensorFlow and PyTorch for training, testing, and deploying music generation models effectively.
- **Music-Specific AI Frameworks**: Frameworks such as Music Transformer are tailored for sequential data processing, enabling the generation of intricate compositions by adapting patterns and structures in music.
- **MIDI Processing Tools**: Libraries like PrettyMIDI and music21 are essential for parsing, analyzing, and generating MIDI data, allowing seamless interaction between musical elements and AI models.
- **Audio Synthesis Engines**: Advanced tools such as WaveNet produce high-quality, realistic audio by transforming model-generated sequences into refined sound outputs.
- **GPU Acceleration**: NVIDIA GPUs play a critical role in expediting the training process of complex neural networks, essential for handling large-scale musical datasets and deep learning tasks.
- **Pre-trained Models**: Leveraging models like OpenAI's Jukebox and AIVA allows developers to fine-tune existing architectures for specific genres, styles, or use cases, saving significant time and resources.
- **Cloud Computing Platforms**: Platforms like Google Cloud AI, AWS SageMaker, and Azure ML provide scalable environments for training and deploying AI music models, offering specialized tools and infrastructure for handling large audio datasets and optimizing computational resources for music generation and analysis.

How Text to Music Models Work

- **Define Input Parameters:** User prompt such as "Create an upbeat workout track with an energetic tempo, electronic beats." This input is tokenized into a format the model can interpret.
- **Data Preprocessing and Augmentation:** The model preprocesses the input by referencing training datasets of similar music styles. It normalizes key features such as tempo, pitch, and rhythm. Additional variations in tempo and instrumentation are introduced during augmentation to improve robustness.
- **Analyze Musical Patterns:** Using its training data, the model identifies patterns common in workout tracks, such as fast tempos, repetitive basslines, and high-energy melodies. Pre-trained embeddings capture relationships between elements like harmony and rhythm, ensuring stylistic consistency
- **Generate Musical Sequences:** Leveraging a Transformer-based architecture, the AI generates sequences of notes and beats, organizing them into phrases that reflect the energetic and motivational tone of workout music. For example, it may create an electronic drum pattern layered with synthesizer melodies.
- **Evaluate and Adjust Output:** The model evaluates the generated music against metrics such as coherence, energy level, and adherence to the "upbeat workout" style. If necessary, reinforcement learning or feedback mechanisms refine the composition.
- **Adapt to Style:** Style transfer techniques are applied to ensure the output aligns with the electronic genre and high-energy tone. Adjustments are made to dynamics and instrumentation, such as adding a driving bassline or increasing tempo to enhance the workout vibe
- **Convert to Audio:** The note sequences are transformed into high-quality audio using synthesis engines.

Real-World Implementations of Text to Music Models

- **Entertainment:** Generate dynamic soundtracks for movies, series, and video games.
- **Advertising:** Create engaging jingles and background music for brand campaigns
- **Education:** Offer interactive tools for teaching music theory and composition.
- **Healthcare:** Produce therapeutic soundscapes for stress relief and wellness.
- **Social Media:** Enable content creators to enhance videos with personalized tracks.
- **Gaming:** Generate adaptive soundtracks that evolve based on gameplay.

AI music models mark a turning point in creative industries, bridging the gap between technology and artistry. These tools empower musicians, producers, and businesses to create original compositions effortlessly, democratizing access to professional-grade music.

As AI continues to evolve, it holds the potential to unlock new frontiers in auditory storytelling, enabling a deeper emotional connection with audiences across the globe.

Data and Cloud

CHAPTER TEN

DATA SCIENCE

Data Science is an interdisciplinary field that merges statistics, computer science, and domain expertise to extract meaningful insights from structured and unstructured data. In today's digital era, where vast amounts of data are generated every second, data science is crucial for uncovering hidden patterns, solving complex problems, and enabling data-driven decision-making. Its applications span diverse industries such as healthcare, finance, retail, and technology, fostering innovation and transforming how businesses operate.

An AI-Generated Illustration of Data Science

Understanding Data Science

Data science is a systematic approach to analyzing data for uncovering patterns, deriving insights, and driving strategic decisions. It involves a series of interconnected stages that transform raw data into actionable knowledge:

- **Data Collection:** Data is gathered from various sources such as databases, sensors, social media platforms, and web APIs, ensuring a comprehensive foundation for analysis.
- **Data Cleaning and Preparation:** Inconsistencies are addressed, missing values handled, and the data is transformed into a suitable format, ensuring it is ready for analysis and modeling.
- **Data Integration:** Combining data from multiple sources to ensure consistency and completeness for a unified analysis.
- **Exploratory Data Analysis (EDA):** Statistical techniques and visualization tools are used to examine data distributions, identify trends, detect anomalies, and generate hypotheses.
- **Feature Engineering:** Creating meaningful features from raw data to enhance model performance and predictive power.
- **Modeling and Algorithm Development:** Machine learning algorithms are applied to create predictive or descriptive models that capture underlying data patterns and relationships.
- **Experimentation and Model Validation:** Testing and validating multiple algorithms to ensure robustness and reliability in predictions.
- **Interpretation and Communication:** Analytical findings are translated into actionable insights and communicated to stakeholders using reports, dashboards, or visualizations for effective decision-making.
- **Deployment and Monitoring:** Models are deployed into production environments and continuously monitored to ensure they deliver accurate and reliable outcomes.

Tools and Technologies in Data Science

The data science ecosystem encompasses a wide range of tools and technologies that enable the analysis, interpretation, and utilization of complex datasets:

Programming Languages

- Python known for its simplicity and versatility, Python offers extensive libraries such as Pandas, NumPy, and SciPy for data manipulation and analysis
- **R:** A powerful language for statistical computing and data visualization, favored in academic and research settings.

Data Visualization Tools

- Tools like Tableau and Power BI facilitate the creation of interactive dashboards and insightful visualizations for non-technical stakeholders.
- Libraries such as Matplotlib, Seaborn, and Plotly are widely used for creating detailed visualizations in programming environments.

Machine Learning Frameworks

- TensorFlow and PyTorch support the design, training, and deployment of advanced machine learning models, including deep learning networks.

- Scikit-learn, a go-to library for implementing classical machine learning algorithms and data preprocessing.

Big Data Technologies

- Apache Hadoop enables the storage and processing of large datasets in distributed computing environments.
- Apache Spark offers faster in-memory data processing, making it ideal for iterative machine learning tasks and large-scale analytics.

Cloud Platforms

- Services like AWS, Google Cloud Platform (GCP), and Microsoft Azure provide scalable infrastructure for data storage, processing, and model deployment.
- These platforms integrate with data science tools like Jupyter Notebooks, AutoML, and Kubernetes for seamless workflows

Data Integration and Workflow Orchestration Tools

- Tools like Apache Airflow and Knime automate and orchestrate complex data science pipelines.
- Talend and Informatica enable seamless data integration from multiple sources.

Challenges in Data Science

While data science holds immense transformative potential, it also faces several critical challenges that can impact its effectiveness:

- **Data Privacy and Security:** Analyzing sensitive information requires strict adherence to regulations like GDPR, HIPAA, and CCPA. Ensuring data privacy while deriving insights is a significant challenge, especially in industries like healthcare and finance.
- **Data Quality:** Incomplete, inconsistent, or biased datasets can undermine the reliability of AI models and analytics. Cleaning, preprocessing, and validating data are time-consuming yet essential steps to ensure meaningful and accurate results.
- **Skill Gap:** Data science is inherently interdisciplinary, requiring expertise in programming, statistics, machine learning, and domain-specific knowledge. The shortage of professionals with this unique skill set creates a significant gap in the field.
- **Model Interpretability:** Advanced algorithms, particularly in deep learning, often function as "black boxes," offering little transparency into their decision-making processes. This lack of interpretability can reduce trust, particularly in high-stakes applications like healthcare and criminal justice.
- **Ethical Concerns and Bias Mitigation:** Addressing ethical concerns such as algorithmic bias and ensuring fairness in AI models is critical. Failure to mitigate biases can lead to discriminatory outcomes, eroding trust in data-driven systems.
- **Scalability and Infrastructure:** Processing and analyzing large-scale datasets require substantial computational resources and efficient infrastructure. Scaling workflows to handle massive data volumes often poses logistical and financial challenges.
- **Integration with Business Processes:** Aligning data science initiatives with business goals and integrating insights into decision-making processes remains a challenge.

Future Trends in Data Science

The field of data science continues to evolve rapidly, with emerging trends shaping its trajectory and impact across industries:

- **Automated Machine Learning (AutoML)** : Tools like Google AutoML and AWS SageMaker Autopilot are revolutionizing the field by automating the end-to-end machine learning process. AutoML democratizes AI by enabling non-experts to build and deploy models efficiently, reducing barriers to entry.
- **Advanced Language Models** : The rise of sophisticated natural language processing (NLP) models are transforming how machines understand and generate human language. These models power applications in chatbots, sentiment analysis, and automated content generation.
- **MLOps (Machine Learning Operations)** : The integration of machine learning into operations emphasizes collaboration between data scientists and DevOps professionals. MLOps focuses on managing the entire machine learning lifecycle, including model deployment, monitoring, and scalability.
- **Explainable AI (XAI)** : With the growing complexity of AI models, there is a rising focus on explainable AI to make model decisions understandable to humans. XAI ensures transparency and builds trust, particularly in sensitive domains like healthcare and finance.
- **Real-Time Data Analytics** : The demand for real-time insights is driving advancements in streaming data analytics platforms like Apache Kafka and Spark Streaming. These technologies enable faster decision-making in areas like fraud detection, e-commerce, and dynamic pricing.
- **Big Data and Quantum Computing** : As datasets grow in size and complexity, quantum computing offers the potential to solve computational problems that are infeasible for classical systems, opening new frontiers for data science.

CHAPTER ELEVEN

DATA PREPARATION AND ANNOTATION

Data is the lifeblood of any artificial intelligence (AI) system, and its quality directly determines the performance of the AI models. This chapter delves into the foundational processes of preparing and annotating data, a critical step in building robust AI systems. From collecting raw data to ensuring its accuracy and relevance, this chapter explores how to make data actionable for AI.

An AI-Generated Illustration Data Preparation and Annotation

Data Pipelines - Collection, Cleaning, Preprocessing

Data Collection:

The first step is gathering raw data from various sources

- Publicly available datasets like ImageNet or OpenAI's GPT datasets
- APIs and web scraping tools for domain-specific data.
- Sensors and IoT devices for real-time data collection.

Organizations often rely on automated pipelines for continuous data collection, ensuring scalability and consistency.

Data Cleaning:

Raw data is rarely perfect. Cleaning involves

- Removing duplicates, inconsistencies, and outliers
- Filling in missing values or handling gaps in datasets
- Standardizing formats, such as converting text to lowercase or normalizing numerical data

Data Preprocessing:

Once clean, data is transformed into a usable format

- Tokenizing text data for NLP tasks.
- Resizing images or normalizing pixel values for computer vision.
- Aggregating time-series data for temporal tasks like forecasting.

Annotating and Augmenting Datasets for Specific Tasks

Enhancing dataset quality and diversity through precise labeling and creative transformations to improve AI model training and performance.

Data Annotation

Annotation is the process of labeling data to guide AI models during training. Examples include:

- Tagging objects in images (e.g., labeling cars and pedestrians for autonomous driving).
- Categorizing text (e.g., identifying positive vs. negative sentiment in reviews).
- Annotating audio for speech recognition or translation.

Annotation requires both domain expertise and precision, as errors can lead to biased or inaccurate models.

Data Augmentation

Data augmentation improves datasets by creating new variations of existing data.

- For images, this could mean flipping, rotating, or changing brightness.
- For audio or text, it could involve adding small distortions like background noise or typos.

Example: In a dataset of mountain images, augmentation could involve rotating the images or adjusting brightness to simulate different times of day, helping the model learn better.

Tools for Data Labeling and Management

Efficient annotation and management tools simplify the data preparation process. Popular tools include:

- **Scale AI:** A leading platform for large-scale labeling tasks, particularly for enterprise use.
- **Label Studio:** An open-source tool for annotating text, images, and videos with customizable workflows.
- **SuperAnnotate:** Designed for computer vision tasks, offering collaborative annotation features.
- **Amazon SageMaker Ground Truth:** Provides automated data labeling using machine learning for efficient and scalable annotation.
- **CVAT (Computer Vision Annotation Tool) :** A powerful open-source tool used in annotating video and image datasets for computer vision tasks.

Challenges in Maintaining Data Quality and Consistency

- **Ensuring Consistency:** Data inconsistencies can arise when collecting from diverse sources. Examples include, Different time zones in timestamps for time-series data, Inconsistent labeling practices across annotators.
- **Avoiding Bias:** Bias can be introduced through unbalanced datasets, Uneven representation of genders or races in face recognition datasets, Skewed data in recommendation systems favoring a particular demographic.

Overcoming bias requires representative sampling and regular audits of datasets.

Freelance Opportunities in Annotation and Dataset Creation

Data annotation has created a thriving gig economy. Companies often outsource annotation to freelancers or platforms specializing in crowdsourced data labeling.

Freelance Roles:

- **Image Labeling Specialist:** Tagging objects in photos for AI training.
- **NLP Annotator:** Categorizing and tagging text for sentiment analysis or language models.
- **Audio Transcriber:** Labeling speech data for training voice assistants or transcription systems.

Advances in AI are automating parts of the data preparation process, reducing the manual effort required. Active learning and semi-supervised techniques enable models to assist annotators by predicting labels for easy cases, leaving complex ones for human review. Additionally, synthetic data and generative AI are increasingly supplementing real-world datasets, revolutionizing how data is prepared for training.

Data preparation and annotation form the bedrock of AI development, transforming raw information into valuable resources for model training. With advanced tools, scalable pipelines, and a growing pool of freelance contributors, this field is evolving rapidly to meet the demands of modern AI systems.

CHAPTER TWELVE

Synthetic Data

Synthetic data is artificially created using algorithms and simulations to replicate the characteristics of real-world data. It serves as an alternative to traditional datasets, enabling the creation of large, diverse, and balanced datasets without compromising privacy or requiring extensive manual collection. This approach allows for generating data in underrepresented or sensitive categories. Moreover, synthetic data can be tailored to specific scenarios or edge cases, improving the robustness and accuracy of machine learning systems.

An AI-Generated Illustration of Sythetic Data Generation

Why Synthetic Data is Essential

- **Overcoming Data Scarcity:** In areas like autonomous driving and rare disease diagnosis, gathering sufficient real-world data is often difficult or impractical. Synthetic data fills these gaps by simulating rare or hard-to-capture scenarios, enabling effective model training.
- **Enhancing Privacy:** Industries such as finance and healthcare utilize synthetic data to train AI models while safeguarding sensitive personal information. This approach ensures compliance with privacy regulations like GDPR and HIPAA.
- **Cost and Time Efficiency:** Creating synthetic data is significantly faster and more cost-effective than manual collection and annotation of large datasets, making it an attractive alternative for resource-intensive projects.
- **Improving Dataset Balance:** Synthetic data addresses dataset imbalances by generating underrepresented examples, ensuring fairer representation of diverse scenarios and populations in AI training.
- **Supporting Edge Cases:** Rare or extreme scenarios, such as atypical weather for autonomous vehicles or unexpected medical anomalies, can be generated to strengthen model robustness and adaptability.
- **Expanding Training Possibilities:** Synthetic data allows for creating tailored datasets for specific use cases, enabling experimentation and refinement of AI models in controlled environments.
- **Mitigating Bias:** Real-world data often contains inherent biases that can negatively affect AI models. Synthetic data can be designed to remove or reduce these biases, ensuring fairer and more equitable AI systems.

Techniques for Generating Synthetic Data

- **Physics-Based Simulations:** Create realistic environments for applications like robotics, gaming, and autonomous driving. Example: Simulating traffic conditions for self-driving cars using tools like CARLA or Unity.
- **Agent-Based Simulations:** Model the behavior of entities or individuals, such as consumer interactions in e-commerce or pedestrian movements in urban settings.
- **Generative Adversarial Networks (GANs):** GANs consist of two neural networks—a generator and a discriminator—that work together to produce realistic synthetic data.Example: GANs generate synthetic images of human faces for training facial recognition systems.
- **Variational Autoencoders (VAEs):** VAEs are effective for generating diverse variations of input data while retaining essential characteristics. They are commonly used for tasks like generating synthetic medical imaging datasets for disease detection and diagnosis.
- **Procedural Generation:** Procedural generation relies on predefined rules and algorithms to create data, often used in generating synthetic datasets for virtual environments or speech synthesis. Example: Creating expansive 3D game worlds or voice datasets by varying pitch, tone, and speed.
- **Rule-Based Simulations:** Constructs data using if-then-else logic or constraints to ensure accuracy in fields like finance or healthcare. Example: Generating synthetic financial transaction records for fraud detection systems.
- **Hybrid Approaches:** Combines multiple methods, such as GANs with procedural generation or VAEs with reinforcement learning, for more robust and diverse synthetic data generation.

Tools for Generating Synthetic Data

- **Unity and Unreal Engine:** Widely used platforms for creating photorealistic 3D simulations. These tools are essential for generating realistic environments in autonomous driving, gaming, and robotics training.
- **NVIDIA Omniverse:** A powerful tool for generating synthetic data, featuring physics-based simulations and realistic environments. It supports a wide range of industries, including robotics, manufacturing, and autonomous vehicles.
- **CARLA and Synthia:** Open-source platforms specializing in creating traffic simulations for training self-driving cars. These tools provide realistic urban and highway scenarios, pedestrian behaviors, and weather conditions for robust AI model development.
- **Gretel.ai:** Offers privacy-preserving synthetic data solutions for sensitive industries like healthcare, finance, and insurance. It focuses on generating datasets that ensure regulatory compliance while maintaining data utility.
- **Datagen:** Specializes in creating human-centric synthetic datasets, such as facial recognition, pose estimation, and activity tracking. These datasets are commonly used in augmented reality (AR), virtual reality (VR), and biometric applications.
- **Blender:** An open-source 3D creation tool widely used for generating synthetic images and animations. Blender's customization and scripting capabilities make it ideal for training AI in visual recognition tasks, such as object detection and segmentation.
- **Synthesia:** Focuses on creating synthetic video datasets, especially for training models in facial recognition, lip synchronization, and avatar generation.
- **Replica Studios:** Specializes in generating synthetic voice data and speech patterns.

Applications of Synthetic Data in AI

- **Autonomous Vehicles:** Synthetic traffic data simulates various road conditions, pedestrian behaviors, and rare scenarios to train self-driving cars.
- **Healthcare:** Synthetic patient records and diagnostic images enable the training of medical AI systems without compromising sensitive data. Example: Generating synthetic MRI scans for cancer detection research.
- **Retail and E-commerce:** Virtual product catalogs and synthetic customer behavior datasets enhance personalized recommendations and marketing strategies.
- **Robotics:** Simulated environments train robots to perform tasks like object manipulation and navigation.
- **Natural Language Processing (NLP):** Synthetic text datasets help in training chatbots, translation models, and language understanding systems.
- **Cybersecurity:** Generate attack patterns and system behaviors to train AI in detecting and mitigating cyber threats.
- **Finance:** Synthetic transaction data and fraud patterns help train AI systems for anomaly detection, credit scoring, and risk assessment without exposing sensitive financial information. Example: Creating synthetic transaction histories to test fraud detection algorithms
- **Entertainment and Gaming:** Synthetic datasets support the creation of realistic characters, environments, and interactions in virtual worlds, enhancing the user experience. Eg: synthetic crowd simulations for realistic gaming environments.
- **Agriculture:** Synthetic data supports AI applications in precision farming by simulating crop growth, pest infestations, and weather patterns. Example: Generating synthetic crop health data to train AI for identifying diseases and recommending treatments.

AI IN THE CLOUD

The convergence of Artificial Intelligence (AI) and cloud computing has transformed the technology landscape, enabling organizations to develop, scale, and manage AI applications with unprecedented ease. Cloud platforms provide the computational power, tools, and infrastructure required for AI, removing the need for costly on-premise setups. This democratization of AI ensures that businesses, both large and small, can innovate at scale.

An AI-Generated Illustration of AI in cloud

Core Features of Cloud-Based AI

- **Scalability:** Cloud platforms automatically scale resources up or down, ensuring organizations can efficiently manage fluctuating workloads without the need for over-provisioning or infrastructure maintenance.
- **Global Accessibility:** AI tools and models hosted on the cloud are accessible from anywhere, enabling seamless collaboration across geographically distributed teams and fostering innovation in remote and hybrid work environments.
- **Pre-Built AI Models and APIs :** Cloud providers offer a variety of pre-trained AI models and APIs for tasks such as image recognition, natural language processing (NLP), speech-to-text, and predictive analytics, accelerating AI adoption without requiring in-depth expertise.
- **Cost Efficiency:** The pay-as-you-go pricing model minimizes upfront investments and allows businesses to pay only for the resources they consume, reducing financial barriers for startups and small businesses.
- **Security and Compliance:** Cloud platforms provide enterprise-grade security, encryption, and compliance with regulations like GDPR and HIPAA, ensuring data protection while training and deploying AI models.
- **High-Performance Computing (HPC) :** Cloud platforms leverage GPUs and TPUs to provide the computational power required for training large-scale AI models, making advanced capabilities accessible without specialized hardware.
- **Customizability:** Many cloud services allow businesses to customize AI models by fine-tuning pre-trained models or building new ones, catering to industry-specific needs.
- **AutoML Tools:** Cloud providers offer automated machine learning (AutoML) tools, allowing non-experts to build and deploy AI models with minimal coding, democratizing access to advanced AI technologies.

Top Cloud AI Platforms

Amazon Web Services (AWS)

- Key Features: AWS SageMaker for building, training, and deploying machine learning models; Rekognition for advanced image and video analysis; Polly for converting text into natural-sounding speech.
- Applications: Fraud detection in financial systems, personalized product recommendations in e-commerce, predictive maintenance in manufacturing, and automated content moderation.

Google Cloud AI

- Key Features: Vertex AI for managing end-to-end machine learning workflows; BigQuery ML for integrating machine learning capabilities into SQL queries; AutoML for training custom AI models without extensive coding.
- Applications: Retail analytics for inventory management, sentiment analysis in customer feedback, and healthcare diagnostics using AI-powered imaging tools.

Microsoft Azure AI

- Key Features: Azure Cognitive Services for advanced language, vision, and speech capabilities; Azure Machine Learning for scalable AI model development and deployment; Form

Recognizer for automated document processing.

- Applications: Real-time chatbot solutions for customer engagement, multilingual translation for global businesses, and intelligent document analysis for legal and financial services.

IBM Watson

- Key Features: Watson Assistant for creating conversational AI solutions; Watson Studio for collaborative AI model development and deployment; Watson Discovery for AI-powered search and data insights.
- Applications: Automation of customer service operations, financial risk modeling, and clinical research for drug discovery and personalized treatment plans.

Oracle AI

- Key Features: Oracle Cloud Infrastructure (OCI) AI Services for pre-built models; Oracle Data Science for end-to-end AI workflows; Voice and vision services for custom AI applications.
- Applications: Predictive analytics in supply chain, AI-driven fraud detection, and personalized customer engagement

Alibaba Cloud AI

- Key Features and Applications: PAI for AI model development, Image Search for reverse lookup, and NLP for multilingual processing; used in e-commerce recommendations, image search, and real-time translation.

AI Workflows in the Cloud

- **Data Collection and Storage:** Cloud platforms like AWS S3, Google Cloud Storage, and Azure Blob Storage provide scalable and secure solutions for managing large datasets essential for AI workflows.
- **Data Preprocessing:** Tools like AWS Glue, Google Dataflow, and Azure Data Factory facilitate data cleaning, transformation, and preparation, ensuring high-quality inputs for AI training
- **Model Training:** Platforms such as Vertex AI, SageMaker, and Azure Machine Learning offer robust computational infrastructure, including GPU and TPU support, to efficiently train large-scale AI models.
- **Model Deployment:** Services like Azure Kubernetes Service (AKS), AWS Elastic Beanstalk, and Google Kubernetes Engine (GKE) simplify the deployment of AI models into production environments, enabling scalability and reliability.
- **Performance Monitoring:** Monitoring tools such as AWS CloudWatch, Google Cloud Monitoring, and Azure Monitor ensure optimal resource utilization and track model performance for continuous improvements.
- **Data Security and Governance:** Ensures secure data handling and compliance with regulations like GDPR, HIPAA, and CCPA during AI development. Examples include AWS Identity and Access Management (IAM) for role-based access control, Google Cloud's Data Loss Prevention (DLP) API for safeguarding sensitive information, and Azure Security Center for comprehensive security and compliance management.
- **Model Fine-Tuning and Optimization:** Example Vertex AI and SageMaker offer transfer learning workflows to fine-tune large models like GPT. Azure AutoML optimizes hyperparameters and selects the best-performing model configurations.

Cloud AI Services: Key Capabilities (few listed below)

Cloud AI providers offer a comprehensive suite of tools designed to empower developers and businesses to integrate artificial intelligence into their applications. These services span across various domains, enabling advanced functionalities in language processing, speech recognition, computer vision, and generative AI. Below is an overview of the core capabilities provided by leading cloud providers:

Language

- **Text Analysis:** Enables businesses to extract meaningful insights from text, including sentiment analysis, key phrase extraction, and language detection.
- **Question Answering:** Provides automated responses to user queries by leveraging AI-powered algorithms for accurate information retrieval.
- **Language Understanding:** Facilitates natural language understanding (NLU) to interpret user intents and extract actionable data.
- **Translation:** Offers real-time translation services across multiple languages, fostering seamless communication globally.

Speech

- **Speech Recognition:** Converts spoken words into text with high accuracy, enabling transcription and voice-enabled applications.
- **Speech Synthesis:** Generates natural-sounding speech from text, enhancing interactive user experiences through voice responses.

- **Speech Translation:** Combines speech recognition and language translation to convert spoken words into another language in real-time.
- **Speaker Recognition:** Identifies and verifies speakers based on unique voice characteristics, enhancing authentication and personalization.

Vision

- **Image and Video Analysis:** Allows organizations to analyze visual content for object detection, facial recognition, and activity monitoring.
- **Image Classification:** Categorizes images into predefined classes, enabling automated tagging and organization.
- **Object Detection:** Pinpoints and identifies objects within images and videos, facilitating use cases like surveillance and inventory management.
- **Optical Character Recognition (OCR):** Extracts text from images, making it searchable and editable for applications like digitizing documents.

Generative

- **Generate Text Completions:** Leverages advanced language models to complete sentences, paragraphs, or code snippets based on user input.
- **Image Generation:** Produces custom images from textual descriptions, enabling creative and design-oriented use cases.

Tools for AI Development in the Cloud

- **Kubernetes:** An open-source platform for deploying, managing, and scaling containerized AI applications. Kubernetes is supported by major cloud providers like AWS (EKS), Google Cloud (GKE), and Azure (AKS), enabling efficient orchestration and fault tolerance.
- **Apache Airflow:** A workflow orchestration tool that simplifies the management of complex data and AI pipelines. Airflow integrates with cloud services like Google Cloud Composer and AWS Managed Workflows for Apache Airflow.
- **MLflow:** An open-source platform for managing the end-to-end machine learning lifecycle. MLflow provides model tracking, reproducibility, and deployment capabilities, supported on all major cloud platforms.
- **Hugging Face:** A platform offering pre-trained transformer models and APIs for NLP, vision, and generative AI tasks. Hugging Face integrates with cloud platforms like AWS SageMaker, Google Cloud, and Azure ML for fine-tuning and deploying models in production.
- **Streamlit:** An open-source framework for creating and deploying interactive dashboards and visualizations for AI models. Streamlit allows rapid prototyping of AI applications and integrates easily with cloud infrastructures for scalable deployment.

Career in AI

CHAPTER FOURTEEN

AI ROLES AND CAREER PATHS

AI roles like Data Scientists, Machine Learning Engineers, and AI Researchers have been prominent since the early 2010s, driven by advancements in big data and deep learning. In recent years, new roles such as AI Ethics Specialists, Prompt Engineers, and AI Product Managers have emerged, highlighting the expansion of AI and the opportunities it creates across diverse fields.

An AI-Generated Illustration of AI workforce

Data Scientist

A Data Scientist is a professional who specializes in analyzing and interpreting complex data to extract actionable insights. Often described as a hybrid between a statistician, programmer, and business analyst, Data Scientists play a crucial role in driving decision-making processes across industries. Their expertise in both technical and domain-specific knowledge allows them to solve business problems, optimize operations, and create predictive models to anticipate future trends.

- **Roles & Responsibilities:** Data Analysis, Machine Learning and AI Implementation, Data Engineering and Preprocessing, Predictive Modeling and Algorithm Development, Collaboration and Stakeholder Communication, MLOps and Deployment.
- **Required Technical Skills:** Proficiency in Python, R, SQL, and machine learning frameworks like TensorFlow, PyTorch, and scikit-learn. Experience with Hadoop, Spark, or equivalent for handling large-scale datasets. Familiarity with AWS (SageMaker, Lambda), Azure (Synapse, Databricks), or Google Cloud (BigQuery, Vertex AI) for scalable deployments. Expertise in Tableau, Power BI, or Python visualization libraries like Matplotlib and Seaborn.Strong understanding of statistical modeling, probability, and optimization techniques.
- **Nice-to-Have Skills:** Certification in cloud platforms like AWS, Azure, or GCP. Familiarity with cutting-edge AI tools like OpenAI APIs or industry-specific AI platforms. Knowledge of domain-specific applications, such as manufacturing analytics or marketing attribution. Proficiency with tools for diagramming (Visio, Lucidchart) or project management (JIRA, Azure DevOps).

Machine Learning Engineer

A Machine Learning Engineer is responsible for developing, deploying, and optimizing machine learning models and algorithms that enable systems to learn, adapt, and improve from data. This role serves as a critical bridge between data science, which focuses on model creation and analysis, and software engineering. It requires a robust foundation in programming, proficiency in building and managing data pipelines, and the ability to collaborate closely with cross-functional teams to integrate models and iterate for continuous improvement.

- **Roles & Responsibilities:** Model Development Design, train, and fine-tune machine learning models, MLOps Implementation Build and maintain ML pipelines for scalable model deployment, monitoring, and management. Data Processing Perform data cleaning, preprocessing, and feature engineering to optimize model performance. Integrate ML solutions into existing systems, Deploy trained models into production, Performance Monitoring, debug models.
- **Required Technical Skills:** Expert in Python, with experience in Java / Scala. Hands-on experience with TensorFlow, PyTorch, Scikit-learn, and other ML frameworks. Familiarity with Spark, Hadoop, and cloud data platforms like AWS Sagemaker, Google Vertex AI, and Azure Databricks. Skilled in CI/CD workflows, containerization (Docker, Kubernetes), MLFlow, Strong understanding of statistics, probability, and optimization techniques. Proficiency in tools like Matplotlib, Seaborn, or Tableau for data visualization.
- **Nice-to-Have Skills:** Familiarity with fine-tuning large language models like GPT or BERT. Knowledge of generative models and tools like LangChain and LLAMAIndex. Experience with Infrastructure-as-Code (e.g., Terraform) and distributed systems. Experience in domain-specific applications for developing customized ML solutions.

More AI Roles

Emerging AI roles such as Computer Vision Engineers, NLP Engineers, and AI Product Managers are redefining the tech landscape.

- **Computer Vision Engineer:** Works on AI models for image and video processing tasks..
- **Natural Language Processing (NLP) Engineer:** Works on designing, developing algorithms and models that enable computers to understand, interpret, and generate human language
- **AI Product Manager:** Oversees the development and lifecycle of AI-driven solutions.
- **AI Solutions Architect:** Designs AI systems tailored to client or organizational needs.
- **Prompt Engineer:** Designs and refines prompts for optimal performance of AI models.
- **AI Ethics Specialist:** Ensures fairness, transparency, and compliance in AI applications.
- **AIOps Engineer:** Integrates AI into IT operations for predictive maintenance and anomaly detection.
- **Big Data Engineer:** Prepares large datasets for AI training and analysis.
- **Data Annotator:** Labels and curates data for training supervised machine learning models.
- **AI Policy Advisor:** Works on regulatory frameworks and compliance for AI applications

The rise of specialized AI roles showcases the emergence of new opportunities in the tech sector, with professionals driving advancements in AI across various domains.

135

CHAPTER FIFTEEN

AI - Certifications

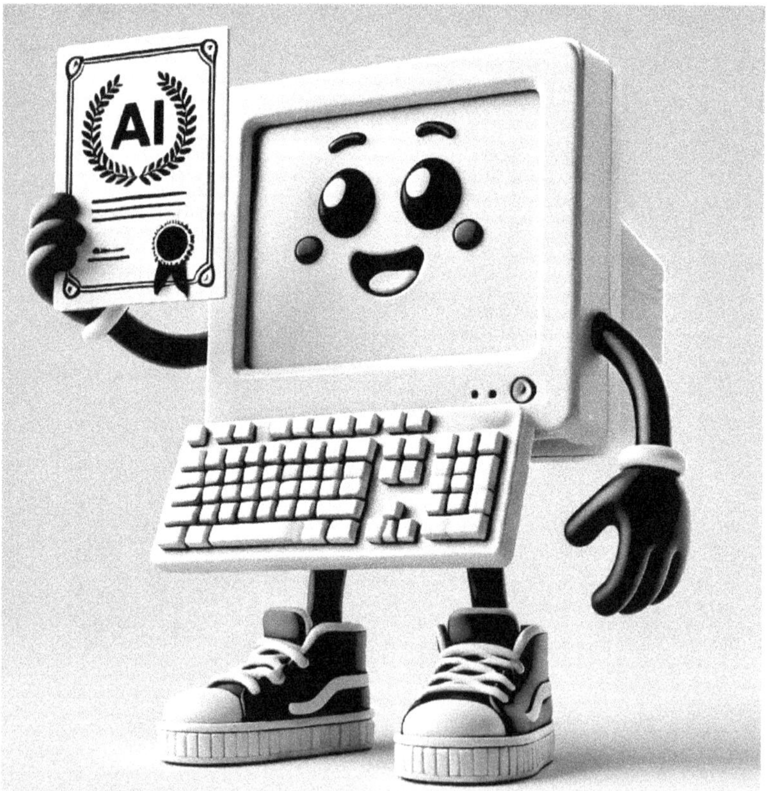

An AI-Generated Illustration of AI Certifications

Available Microsoft Certifications: An Overview

Beginner/Foundational Track

- Microsoft Certified: Azure Fundamentals (AZ-900)
- Microsoft Certified: AI Fundamentals (AI-900)
- Microsoft Certified: Data Fundamentals (DP-900)

Developer Track

- Microsoft Certified: Azure AI Engineer Associate (AI-102)
- Microsoft Certified: Azure Developer Associate (AZ-204)

Data Science and Machine Learning Specialist Track

- Microsoft Certified: Azure Data Scientist Associate (DP-100)
- Microsoft Certified: Azure Data Engineer Associate (DP-203)

Available Amazon Certifications: An Overview

- AWS Certified Cloud Practitioner
- AWS Certified Data Analytics – Specialty

Available IBM Certifications: An Overview

- Data Scientist - Associate (watsonx)
- AI Enterprise Workflow V1 - Specialist
- Administrator - Cloud Pak for Watson AIOps v3.2
- Generative AI Engineer - Associate (watsonx)
- AI Assistant Engineer v1 - Professional (watsonx)
- Data Scientist - Machine Learning Specialist v1
- Data Scientist - Watson Specialist v1

Available Google Certifications: An Overview

- Professional Data Engineer
- Professional Machine Learning Engineer

Listed here are a few professional certifications from major tech companies like Microsoft, IBM, AWS, and Google, designed to equip individuals with expertise in AI, machine learning technologies.

Author Note

Thank you for taking the time to explore AI Deep Dive. It has been an honor to guide you through the fascinating world of Artificial Intelligence. My hope is that this book has not only broadened your understanding of AI but also ignited curiosity and enthusiasm for its transformative role in shaping our future.

Through each chapter, we've seen how AI has developed not only as a technological force but also as a tool that shapes industries, assists in daily tasks, and opens new frontiers for human potential. With AI continuing to grow, the journey of learning and discovery is far from over. Thank you again for taking the time to explore AI's rich history with me—I look forward to the innovations that await us all in the future.

Together, let's embrace the opportunities AI presents and be part of shaping a future driven by innovation and intelligence.

With gratitude..!!

Mohammed Yousef Shaik
AI Entrepreneur and Innovator – Business, Creativity, and Knowledge
2024